Genesis

haibun

Jonathan McKeown

Genesis

copyright © 2022 Jonathan McKeown
ISBN 978-1-947271-91-3

Red Moon Press
PO Box 2461
Winchester VA
22604-1661 USA
www.redmoonpress.com

cover photograph by Andy MacLean

first printing

For Els

❦

. . . recalling the passage in which Elijah the prophet says, *the Lord . . . lives, before whom I stand today . . .* [Antony] observed that in saying today he [Elijah] was not counting the time passed, but as one always establishing a beginning, he endeavoured each day to present himself as the sort of person ready to appear before God . . .

— Athanasius[1]

But there with all the jackals, panthers, hounds,
The monkeys, scorpions, the vultures, snakes,
Those howling, yelping, grunting, crawling brutes,
The infamous menagerie of vice,

One creature only is most foul and false!
Though making no grand gestures, nor great cries,
He willingly would devastate the earth
And in one yawning swallow all the world;

He is Ennui! — with tear-filled eye he dreams
Of scaffolds, as he puffs his water-pipe.
Reader, you know this dainty monster too;
— Hypocrite reader, — fellowman, — my twin!

— Charles Baudelaire [2]

---

1. Athanasius: *The Life of Anthony and the Letter to Marcellinus*.
2. 'To the Reader' in *The Flowers of Evil*.

The human being is a synthesis of the psychical and the physical, but a synthesis is unthinkable if the two are not united in a third. This third is spirit. In innocence . . . spirit is present, but as immediate, as dreaming. So far as it is now present, it is in a sense a hostile power, for it constantly upsets the relation between soul and body . . . It is, on the other hand, a friendly power that wishes precisely to constitute the relation.

— Vigilius Haufniensis[1]

A human being is a synthesis of the infinite and the finite, of the temporal and the eternal, of freedom and necessity, in short, a synthesis. A synthesis is a relation between two. Considered in this way, a human being is still not a self.

— Anti-Climacus [2]

. . . one cannot arrive at being — one can only start with it.

Nicolas Berdyaev[3]

Accidie is there every time one begins something . . .

— Abba Poemen (called the Shepherd) [4]

---

1. One of Kierkegaard's 'lower' pseudonyms. *The Concept of Anxiety*.
2. One of Kierkegaard's 'higher' pseudonyms. *The Sickness Unto Death*.
3. Nicolas Berdyaev, *The Destiny of Man*.
3. *The Sayings of the Desert Fathers*, in 'Poemen (called the Shepherd)'.

Genesis

A Tree

And God called the vault Heavens.

— Genesis 1:8

I am in Northern Queensland visiting my brother and his wife who've just had their first baby. The occasion is also an excuse for me to take a short holiday. I have brought Bashō's *Travel Sketches* with me and this morning, amidst unusual bird chatter and the intermittent yapping of a gecko in the rafters, I began to read *A Visit to the Kashima Shrine* where I came upon this haiku published under the pen name of Tosei but composed while Bashō was at the shrine:

> in the days
> of the ancient gods,
> a mere seedling
> this pine must have been.

It put me in mind of a gigantic dead gum tree that was still standing on my parent's farm when they bought it more than forty years ago. I was only three. From our big kitchen window we had a good view of the property — despite its always being smeared with horse saliva. The big old tree stood only fifty meters or so from the house but (perhaps because it was dead) you could easily look right past it as your eye ran out to some more distant feature: the dam with its circle of reeds, or the row of old pine trees on the far hill that marks the border of the property — so present it was almost invisible. But there it always stood: its bleached grey branches, rooted in the sky, defying the winds.

I moved back to the farm with some friends when I was in my thirties. We hadn't been there long when my girlfriend's dog went wandering. I thought I could hear him yelping in the direction of a farmhouse across the valley, so I paid a visit to the neighbours. Sure enough they had found Zeus and put him in one of their pig-pens for safe keeping. We got to talking over a cup of tea and the woman brought out an old photograph that was taken four years before I was born — looking back to (what then was not yet) our farmhouse on the hill. In the distance you could see the very same familiar old tree standing there, still dead in 1963. They say it was struck by lightning, but there is no living soul that could say for sure. It stood another fifty years or so before eventually it fell. My father was living there alone at the time. But no-one saw it fall, or heard it fall. He just discovered its great body lying there one morning after something strange about the sky made its absence felt.

Recently my father sold the farm. While I was helping him move I took one last walk around the place. I found the carcass of that old tree: the birds had covered it in blackberry.

>   endless sky
>   my first thought
>   of eternity

gas guns punctuating the crowless sky

rural blue a small plane cuts its engine

Home

> "... *cursed be the soil for your sake* ..."
> — Genesis 3:17

They'd pulled the old farm house down. The once grand pepper tree still stood, decrepitly. Long grass grown up around the old tractor in the paddock. I found the remains of the porch swing, buckled, rusting, tangled in the wire of our old prop clothesline. The tank-stand, now tankless, standing still ... The rhythmic clunking of water hammer in pipes pumping from the dam came back to me clearly as if it were pumping still ... Bits of farm machinery ... other things I'd forgotten ... fragments of childhood ... half buried ...

>hearthstone
>redolence of a flower
>I cannot find

Blue Glue

*As you went stooping with your barrow full
Into an absolution of the body . . .*

— Seamus Heaney, 'The Gravel Walks'

For me it's not so delicate or refined as a dainty piece of madeleine dipped in her decoction of lime-blossom tea; it's the strong, distinct yet pleasant smell of what my father called "blue glue"—the solvent cement we use to join pipes and fittings made of PVC. Even today, absorbed in the work at hand, a half-oblivious whiff did the trick; wafting over from the apprentice repairing the stormwater service at the top of the steep driveway of a house in Church Point. I stood gazing down toward the yachts in the marina, but I was looking down on a vista of memory: the mound of blue-metal, the wheel-barrow and shovel, the earth-heaped banks of trenches and bridges of planks, and me trying to keep up with my father laying a run of pipe. The whole vivid, grey-bleak scene opened up before me: the half-built house in a clearing of trees out the back of Portland somewhere, and Dad and me working against the light and rain to be home for the weekend. I'd be exaggerating to make it seem *the vast structure of recollection* to which that smell is key were accessible only by heroic labours of poetic subtlety, a la Proust, sipping his cup of tea *in search of lost time*. Some men's minds so utterly are in their bodies, their hands—their tools . . .

    sleet-stinging drizzle
    the shove of the spade
    in the pipe-bed of gravel

Inheritance

> *The autobiography of an old board is a kind of literature not yet taught on campuses . . .*
>
> — Aldo Leopold, *A Sand County Almanac*

"This really is a beautiful table," she says, running her hand over its surface during a lull in the conversation. Her brother-in-law is opening another bottle of wine and doesn't respond.

"There's a bit of a story behind it," his wife says, taking up the slack.

"Do tell . . ." she says to her brother-in-law, focussed now on pouring. His wife continues:

"Charlie's Dad's younger brother — Uncle Dan — had the idea to make it out of some old timber from the original slab-house at the Farm — wasn't it?"

"Ironbark," says Charlie.

"Apparently he wanted to make this huge round table like King Arthur's so the whole family could feast around it at Christmas and family get-togethers. But he never finished it . . . his girlfriend left him or something and he lost the motivation. Charlie said it weighed a tonne and looked like a gigantic wagon wheel when his Dad started working on it. It had all these rough-cut timbers around this central disc," she said, circling it with her hand. "They look like the rays of the sun, don't you think? . . . Apparently it sat out at the Farm for — what was it, Charlie? — ten years or something? — 'til we had to sell it — the Farm that is. That's when Charlie's Dad got a notion and moved it to his shed so he could work on it. But he wasn't sure about the design. Charlie says he got the idea of squaring it like this from his older brother (I never met him) — the post-and-rail style legs too — like the post-and-rail fences at the Farm. It's a bit hard to picture it now but they reckon it looks heaps better square than it did round. Isn't that right?"

Charlie nodded, though it was more of a slow blink.

"Anyway, Charlie's Dad was the one that finished it," she said. "He did a beautiful job. Most of the time we don't even think about it, though we eat off it every day; it's just there like the floor or the sky, you know. But there are moments . . . when the kids are at school and the house is quiet . . . when its presence . . . when I appreciate the company of something so wise . . ."

> growing up
> around an old ironbark
> a ring of saplings

Mt Isa

... and there was light. And God saw the light, that it was good, and God divided the light from the darkness ...

— Genesis 1:3, 4

This was not waking up — not as I in my short life had known it. Waking entails the *ineluctable modality of the visible: at least that if no more.* But this morning — that morning — only *thought* (though not) *through my eyes.* The world — in that modality — lost to me. Dreadful thought. I get up — got up — feeling my way through space   between objects in a space   objects no longer there   visibly: pillow   bedhead   sheet   floor my place in the felt — in the echoing — space of things between things   reorienting. My dark modalities tentatively creep — crept — out of hiding, making new sense of things, new sense of waking: the door   the hall Mummy and Daddy's room   door knob   their bed their smell   their breathing   Mummy's voice ...

> drinking from the pool
> of an old dog's eye
> a ring of flies

Horizons

. . . and God's breath hovering over the waters . . .
— Genesis 1:2

I live my life in out-growing rings . . .
— Rilke, The Book of Hours I.2

I'll never forget the first time I took you to Maroubra, he said, leaning on one of those treated-pine fenceposts, towel around his neck, non-matching thongs on his feet. He's unsteady as a toddler these days, stopping at intervals to catch his breath. Nothing stops him talking though: It was when we were living at Mt Isa. Just after your brother was born. You were just a little kid. We'd driven back to Sydney to show him to your grandparents. It was a nice sunny day like this when we dropped in so I left your baby brother and your mother with her parents at Oatley and took you to the beach. We were walking up this track, somewhere around here — though it was a bit different then — there weren't all these fences. We were coming over the sand dunes right about here when you heard the waves and looked and saw the water and stopped dead in the track. "Dad!" you said. "Look at that big dam!"

>   summer's end
>   gull prints
>   in the concrete

creek bank
she christens the turtle
we came to release

Exposure

Their eyes were opened, and they knew that they were naked...

— Genesis 3:7

I remember one morning as a child waiting for the school bus at our front gate. After a while our neighbours pulled up in their four-wheel-drive: "The bus's already gone, Darlin'. Do you wanna lift?" I climbed in. Her daughter smiled and slid across. I don't recall now what was said on the way. I remember liking how high it felt up in the front seat. Most vividly I remember arriving at school — how distressed I felt — when instead of parking out on the street like the school bus she pulled into the driveway of the main gate and continued driving right up to the edge of the playground — brimming like a sea of glistening eyes. I didn't understand then why I did what I did — pretending to be goofing off — not to seem rude I suppose — I slipped to the floor like a fish and even before the vehicle came fully to a halt — already had the door open — just enough to let myself out like water through the crack and disappear in that ocean of anonymity.

> first shiver
> nothing at the centre
> of the spreading rings

Peaches and Cream

> *Being begins with well-being.*
> — Gaston Bachelard, *The Poetics of Space*

> *. . . cursed shall you be by the soil that gaped with its mouth . . .*
> — Genesis 4:11

The milking songs in Carmichael's *Carmina Gadelica* take me back to my childhood, to our little farm at Silverdale, and the two milking cows my mother named Buttercup and Daisy. My brother and I used to call them up in the mornings. We'd sometimes watch Dad wash their pink freckled udders and teats with a soft muslin cloth that he'd rinse and wring with his hands in a bucket of warm water before he set to milking. I remember the rhythmic sound the milk would make squirting into the bucket.

> dusk deep in the valley of a cow's falsetto

Number 99, titled simply 'Milking song', I find especially moving and consult the notes at the end. Carmichael says these songs were sung to induce the cows to give their milk, that some became so accustomed to a milkmaid's lilt that without it they'd refuse. Our science and technologies have come a long way, but reading things like this one can't help feeling something also has been lost . . . The delight I felt as a child, sitting in the shade of the barn on a hot summer afternoon with a bucket of over-ripe peaches that Mum had collected from under the trees. The sweetness of her voice in her songs as she pared away bruised bits from the stones is so mingled now in memory as the aroma of ripe peaches with those juicy bits of flesh she handed each of us in turn.

>   still life
>   a bowl of fruit
>   with little stickers

fossil fuels a dream beyond the hood of a day moon

Jim Brown

The Nephilim were on the earth in those days...
— Genesis 6:4

He was a man I didn't really know, being only a kid. People said he was an old coal miner. I remember some things: his stature, and his voice, but his face has faded. He lived on a large property out the back of Lithgow, though the bounds of it were never really clear to me. Everyone called it Brown's Farm. He let church and community groups use it for weekend camps and retreats. We stayed there maybe half a dozen times growing up. There was this old shearing shed he'd converted to a bunk-house. It had a large dining room with trestle tables, a kitchen, and a big fireplace in the middle that forty or more people could sit around and often did, due to the weather. I can almost feel the sting of sleet on my face and knuckles just remembering, riding around on the back of the old flat-bed truck... and smell the coal smoke that hung in the air. There was an old boiler we had to light a fire under early in the morning if we wanted hot showers, and there were horses we would ride, and a black dog that came around sometimes, and a lot of other things. But I only remember meeting him once...

My brother had managed to get his four-wheel-drive bogged to the axles hooning about in a sodden paddock. We tried for hours to get it out before someone asked about the old bulldozer parked a little way off on the rise of a hill...

My brother looked like a child beside him as he lumbered down the slope to the edge of the bog where we were waiting. He surveyed our predicament for a moment, before turning slowly and heading up the hill toward the dozer. You couldn't help feeling the tension Jim Brown's inscrutable silence seemed to generate as my brother rabbited on: "It's in pretty deep. . . . We've been tryin' for ages. . . . We tried towin' it out with that other four-wheel-drive. Everything. . . . D'ya think that'll be able to pull it out?" he said, apprehensive at the mud-caked dozer as he gave way at last to the big man's over-bearing silence and waited for him to say something. . . .

There was only a brief pause before Jim Brown responded, and when he did he spoke slow and calm, deliberate, his voice impressive: deep and clear, resounding, like the voice of a giant:

"Well," he said, hoisting himself into the saddle of the mechanical beast, "it'll pull it out, or pull it in halves."

> early flight
> a jumbo rumbles
> a fledgling's sky

distant lightening
the pin-wheel in the planter box
starts to putter

The Flood

The rain fell on the earth forty days and forty nights.
— Genesis 7:12

Our headlights skimmed the swollen river beyond the barricades at Wallacia. The bridge we'd crossed only hours before was somewhere beneath the brown swirling surface. Dad wound down his window to men with torches in yellow rain coats. They said we could try going the long way round. But we found the bridge at Camden under too. So we headed back up the Mountains, to the home of the people we'd had dinner with earlier that evening.

When we arrived the adults returned to the living room and to their conversation. My brother and I found a teenage boy, who must have come home while we were away, watching a movie in their TV room. He barely acknowledged us when we peered in tentatively at the doorway, but giving no sign of objection we crept in and sat down quietly watching . . .

a woman being chased through her house by a tough, tenacious, knife-wielding little monster with pointy, razor-sharp teeth . . . a tense, suspenseful struggle in which she eventually manages to trap it in the oven and cook it till it's smoking, dead. I begin to relax as she picks up the telephone — hands still trembling — and dials a friend. He's coming straight over. Seeming relieved, she catches her breath, surveying the scene, her eyes coming to rest on the kitchen knife the little monster had dropped in the tussle. She picks it up, squats down, assuming the same freaky posture of her attacker. The movie ends — with her mindlessly stabbing the floor, a malevolent grin spreading, deforming her face in anticipation . . .

but it doesn't — end. My brother and I are put to bed on air-mattresses in the lounge-room of this strange house with its dark doorways and halls, long drapes, and unfamiliar, creaking sounds. Outside, I can hear it . . . the rain, unrelenting.

>   to and fro of a raven
>   overture to a rainbow's
>   full circle

mossy stone
the people that built
this forgotten weir

The Dell

"Let the waters under the heavens be gathered..."
— Genesis 1:9

It was strange to see him in the kitchen, Dad mixing flour and water, adding a little salt and sugar, kneading and rolling it into a ball. He put it in a Tupperware container, then raided Mum's sewing box for a reel of cotton and some pins. We just need some pliers and a box of matches. Come on then...

We followed him along the track that led from our house through the tall gum trees, past the old burnt-out car, to Aunty Vi's, but kept on going. My little brother asked lots of questions; but I listened, not wanting to miss anything: — where we were going — what the place was like — what we'd be doing. Crossing Mt York Road he found a barely visible track I'd never noticed that trailed off into the bush. Now keep your eyes peeled for a nice straight stick, one each, about yea big . . . The track got steeper and steeper still but we were on a mission, bringing what we'd gleaned: Like this? No, longer. This? That'll do. We followed him down to a dark pool, out along the top of the stone wall someone had built to dam it. He squatted on his haunches, and with the pliers bent some pins into fishhooks, broke matchsticks in half for floats and tied them to the cotton, the cotton to our sticks. Bring 'em 'ere, he said, opening the lid and pinching off a bit of dough, showing us how to squeeze it round our hooks. Now hang 'em down in the water — but keep an eye on the matchstick. Wait till they're nibbling, and when the match goes under — jag it a bit and pull'em up. That's what we did. First watch the little bits of dough plop and sink, fading into the deep, then stare at our match-floats jiggling at the centre of the spreading rings. It wasn't long before my brother pulled one in — the little gold fish that lived in the black deep. Then me. And so it went, all afternoon. Dad and my brother and me fishing from the wall. Pulling up one after another and setting them free, and watching them wriggle down and disappear in darkness. An eternity might have passed for all we knew. As if through the twilight of the Dell we'd passed unwittingly into another world. When hunger began to gnaw in our bellies we too nibbled at the dough. At last the chill of the descending dew broke the spell and our thoughts turned to home.

> wood smoke
> through moonlit trees
> the light of a house

Initiation

*... This one at last, bone of my bones
and flesh of my flesh ...*

— Genesis 2:23

And I from childhood worshipped in the cult ...

— Baudelaire, 'Lesbos'

I don't remember many girls from primary school but I remember Sappho. She was not like other creatures. She had a strange allure: petite, a slightly exotic complexion augmented by the pale blue of her uniform, and playful, daring eyes. I can still picture her standing there, as if on a stage, in front of the Principal's office one morning — before his impending arrival like clockwork when he would pick some eager kid to ring the old bell to mark the beginning of a new school day ...

    one   two   three   four

A new school day. Fronting her little coterie of friends — like the back-up singers of her band — she struck a precocious stance: humouring us — as adults sometimes do with children, bored with their desire for repetition; knowing she had something boys — *and* girls, in different ways — desire ...

    sorry boys

Desire. At that ingenuous age I couldn't have said what it was, but sensed somehow that she enjoyed it. Who wouldn't? — being worshipped. — That feeling of power — of glory; basking in the ardour of her spellbound neophytes. My friends accosted me at the gate when I arrived and brought me before her, entreating her to show me too . . .

    no more

Esau

The children struggled together within her . . .
— Genesis 25:22

We were not like Chang and Eng Bunker, the Siamese Twins. I can only begin to imagine . . . — what it was like for their wives, the Yates sisters, making love; or taking a shit; attached to Chang while he was drunk or coughing from bronchitis day and night, bedridden while his brother recovered from a stroke, let alone waking up to find him dead — to feel his death seeping through . . . I was not even a twin. I was the firstborn in a household that, relatively speaking, never got any bigger — at times, in fact, it felt like it was shrinking. I always had to 'make room', to accommodate another sibling. For me every multiplication and addition meant another division and subtraction. I had to share a room, a bunk-bed, a whole lot of things with my brother from the time he was born until I left home. We lived in a caravan and a modified tractor shed most of my childhood. We fought a lot; friction was inevitable, I see that now. He pissed me off sometimes. My mother tried to mediate but it was my father I blamed. I don't blame him anymore. Home was another womb . . . a matter of time before the labour pains began . . .

> nectaring
> the spring-back
> of the firespike flute

stealing
over the moon-silvered rooves
the shadow of a reindeer

Lucifer on Third Street

We returned to our places, these Kingdoms,
But no longer at ease here, in the old dispensation
— T. S. Eliot, 'Journey of the Magi'

Christlike cadence of the Magi's breathless descent

When I was a child this gaudy ritual was unthinkable. Not just the glare of neon candy canes, the hallucinatory overlay of laser projections, the strobing technicoloured LEDs; supervening fluorescent facades transforming homes, streets, neighbourhoods — even our antipodean season — into a burlesque carnival of sideshow alleys. Children, cheeks as ruddy as bacchanalian fauns', easily assume entitlements that were at that age unimaginable to me.

hemming his realm of infinite possibility . . . little star

I remember walking up the slow-stepped garden path, bathed in streetlight and the scent of geranium, toward the broad sandstone steps of my grandparent's house on Ada Street in Oatley, and receiving in that moment an indelible impression: through the flawed, bleary panes of one of their bay windows, within the darkened living room: warm-coloured cheery little cone-shaped bulbs softly blinking on the tree: blinking   blinking   blinking with just enough   between   to feel   the absence   of light.

a manger near the queue to the soft-serve van

calla lily
mud spattered
on the spathe

Mycelium

. . . she was the mother of all that lives.
— Genesis 3:20

. . . I am referring . . . to being which is still dark . . .
— Berdyaev, *The Destiny of Man*

As a kid you never suspect . . . the vast invisible network beneath your feet. They're just there, after rain; then gone again. Natural parts of the world that come and go without saying. You don't consider them as 'fruit' or think of what strange 'tree'. The countless times I said "penicillin", when doctors asked if I had allergies, without the slightest inkling or curiosity . . . I first began to wonder when I noticed those magical-looking red-and-white spotted ones — the same that used to pop up beneath the row of old pine trees at our farm — growing miles away in the mountains, beneath a similar row of trees. And this old guy at church, Doc Aberdeen. I thought he was just a normal kind of doctor, even after I went to his home. Paintings of all kinds of bizarre and brightly colored fungi were hung on every wall. "My wife paints these," he said, when he noticed me looking. Even so, it wasn't till his funeral that I learned he was a doctor of mycology . . . that his wife used to illustrate the specimens he collected . . .that he'd been hospitalized several times after sampling minute quantities . . .

> mushroom picking
> something about his mother
> he never knew

The Philosopher's Stone

The inner self ... is like a very shy wild animal that never appears whenever an alien presence is at hand ...
— Thomas Merton, *The Inner Experience*

In the moment actuality is posited, possibility walks by its side as a nothing that entices every thoughtless man.
— Kierkegaard, *The Concept of Anxiety*

I'm sitting with some people around a camp fire — roughly where the old stricken tree would have been — when out of the surrounding darkness he enters the firelight — my brother, a little boy again — wanting me to follow him ...

He leads me down the gully, to the hole in the creek, and shows me the way in ... Getting down on my hands and knees I crawl up the small trickle of the creek through overhanging ferns and bracken into a kind of grotto, a secluded pool. To my left, out the corner of my eye something on the bank moves — startled: a grey water dragon, poised, its wary eye on me. Though common here, this one's legs are strange, tiny and unformed. But it has this perfect, multi-faceted diamond balanced impossibly, sort of hovering, at the tip of its nose. In a blink it's gone — back into the pool ... but what re-emerges from the dark water on the opposite bank is something different, or changed: a snake with multiple heads, bible-black. One of its glossy eyes captures mine, and for a moment we regard one another ...

I return to the fire to tell the others, and a mysterious woman in a grey hooded cloak, shadowed by an auxiliary male, steps forward, taking it upon herself to investigate the veracity of my story . . .

When they return she tells the rest — that remained huddled around the fire — that they'd seen nothing — implying my fabulous story was nothing but a dream. Feeling I have no credibility among these docile people I hold my peace and everyone begins settling down to sleep. But as the shrouded woman reclines I catch a glimpse of her foot in the firelight: in its arch a large reddish-brown swelling the size of an apple but all cracked-looking like sun-scorched clay . . .

>   muttering flames
>   beyond the dwindling
>   circle of light

morning fog
throwing a cricket
off its song

Dungeon

. . . and he dreamed, and, look, a ramp was set against the ground with its top reaching the heavens . . .

— Genesis 28:12

My mother and I are sitting in silence on the sandstone steps of my Grandparent's house in Oatley. She's just put her mother in a nursing home and is still going through a difficult property settlement after leaving my father. My life has also run aground. And to top it off I'm afraid the woman I'm in love with is wanting to leave me. Talking about it is futile. So weighed down, both of us just sit, sunken in ourselves. I remember something . . . and tell her for the sake of conversation:

I had a dream last night that I was at aunty Jan and uncle Robert's old orchard at Glenorie. I was watching Zeus — the dog — sniffing around as if he was on the trail of something when he disappeared behind the shrubs at the side of the house. I went around after him and found an opening to a passage that descended in a spiral of stone stairs. They led down to an empty dungeon. But when I got to the bottom Zeus was nowhere to be seen. I went to leave but the stairs had turned to a steep, slippery ramp, and though I tried repeatedly I couldn't get traction. I was wondering how to escape when Zeus suddenly reappeared and without even thinking — followed him. Before I knew it I was back up, outside in the open air.

That reminds me of when you were a little boy, when we were living in Mt Isa. I don't know if you remember, you were very little, but all around the caravan where we lived there were these low desert shrubs. One day I remember seeing something moving a little way off in the distance. As I watched I realised it was you. I was surprised at how far away you were from the van so I kept my eye on you. I was curious what you were up to. You did this big circuit and as you got nearer to the caravan our black kelpie, Tassie, emerged from behind the shrubs a little way in front of you. I realised then you must have been following her.

>through a rust hole
>in the tractor shed roof
>a shaft of light

Mt Solitary via The Ruined Castle

"A restless wanderer shall you be on earth."
— Genesis 4:12

Deep in the canyon I come upon a little patch of sunlight on the rainforest floor and sit and pour myself a cup of tea. The track notes are sketchy. I think I've missed it. Maybe the turn-off was overgrown. In my mind I retrace my steps, the way I've come, wondering at the possibilities. Should I back-track? The day's getting away. I zip my pack and press on. . . .

> somewhere between
> the currawong's shadow
> and the winter sun

travel journal
the texture of a page
grazed by sunlight

Ganga

... a river flows out of Eden ...

— Genesis 2:10

Banaras: the subtle glamour dawn's smoky light spread across her expansive skin. Even before the blazing crimson disc emerged, new-born, exotic perfumes are mingled with indigoes, translucent salmon-flesh, lava in purple velvet, mauves in lemon-glows. The spell is broken though: the grinning boatman draws attention to something lifted on his oar: a dead baby, its skin muddled hues of silty bronze and grubby brown, breaches, rolls and slips back down...

Laksman Jhoula: in the Himalayan foothills her swift waters are milky jade. Half an hour's walk up-stream, sitting on a sandy beach among the litter of pleasure-seeking backpackers, soaking up the last warmth of the afternoon sun, watching the few remaining bathers, considering one last dip before the sun departs behind the looming mountains—a young man launches from the water. His movement unusual, excessive somehow,—flinging arms and water in the air and falling back as if performing some dramatic death scene... but doesn't come up...

> cold mountain shadow
> only a backpack
> left on the beach

30 year reunion
my old mates discuss
pork belly

full moon
a shadow of the man
that hasn't been

Lowlands

... Then he became the builder of a city ...
—Genesis 4:17

Tonight the reverie follows that soaring sound again, through back-alleys and car-less corridors of a dreaming city. Mere mortal breath cannot release the peculiar timbre of the heart-reed. It steals in to the drunk, bizarre—the piper's haunting call—searching the heart-streets... Strange vivid footsteps, scuffing, boots down there on swinging feet. The wind's cold fingers feeling for the blood-warm skin. Thumbing smooth-worn serrations—a key—in a pocket. Close-sounding—swept away. Suddenly to come upon him, standing in the shadowed alcove—penumbra of an unremembered dream—the solitary vigilant sporran-kilted piper gazing beyond, sending out that proud mournful bracing sound into the soul of my sleeping city.

> single malt
> the circle cast
> by firelight

apart from her moonlight on the calla lilies

shortening days
light from the windows
of inbound trains

Windhover

> *... the earth then was welter and waste and darkness over the deep and God's breath hovering ...*
>
> —Genesis 1:1

... Desolate. In the Mountains by myself. In that house I rented — in the same town. As if I was the only person left on earth ... and the only thing I could think about was her ... out there somewhere. For months I consoled myself by performing the rites ... alone — the cigarettes, the joints — the last vestiges, the sacraments of our 'sixties'. Every night just smoking, staring at the fire ... trying to see a future, or a way back, to somehow escape the dungeon of my life ... Life. It wasn't life. But I was stubborn, like a sulky child. That's where perdition begins: clinging to a corpse of used-to-be; refusing to be consoled by anything else ...; the sickness of the dead that don't yet know it. Eventually it infects your mind — the morbid logic. That's when I started 'ideating' ... you know —

So what happened? I mean, evidently you didn't — you know ...

A strange thought ... more like a voice — the way it entered, but quiet ... like Gerard Manley Hopkins muttering, indistinguishable from the fire — those *blue-bleak embers* ... (— Do you know it? —) ... *fall, gall themselves, and gash gold-vermillion*[1] ... No matter how hopeless my life seemed ... and though I couldn't believe, I couldn't actually once-and-for-all deny — the possibility ... — of hope, I suppose; of a good beyond that of my own

---
1. 'The Windhover'.

monotonous desire . . . Do you know what I mean? — If possibility existed, tomorrow, next year, who knows . . . In a certain respect it's easy to deny, but somehow . . .

    dead wood
    the ministry
    of wind

malingering
in a sunless hollow
autumn dew

golden orb
the weight of dew
in the web

Sense of Humour

... the wish is the consolation ... disconsolateness invents ...
— Kierkegaard, *Without Authority*

Waking groggily, trying to place the faint static sound coming from everywhere ... nowhere.

>thresholdsoftmorningrainontheroof

The cloud cover humidity drags me hot and sweaty from sleep. Night leaving me to face another day. Unreadily lingering, detained in remembrance ... of the funny Do List I'd seen, lying on the table at her mother's. My daughter's lists, unlike mine, are of things she looks forward to. Such untainted expectancy, strange to me now, insubstantial as a shadow, as a memory of a childhood holiday ...

>dawn breakers
>from my bunk in our van
>first day ...

Is it naïve — believing life will keep its promises? What are the dreams of children if not the promises life whispers? Somewhere I drifted across the threshold — the far horizon of my childish dreams — into this harbour of forgotten seas. Battered by storms, making dreary lists of things to do against the tendency to neglect what must be done. Harbour of dead dreams, of desiccated dreams; harbour where old men no longer dream, or suffer little children to ...

>morning fog
>the element in the jug
>begins to crackle

wave
after
wave
my
un-
done
to-
do
list

the image
in which I form
the body of our snow-woman

the long   drive   home
between   alpine   peaks
half-a-dozen sunsets

morning rush
waiting for the honey
to run

post-winter
blackbird
has spoken

The Monk's Rosary

> *... and he took one of his ribs and closed over the flesh where it had been ...*
>
> — Genesis 2:21

It was the title I'd given a selection of music tracks I'd made for her more than five years ago. Desire the thread that pulled them together. A reply of sorts to her last letter; the title italicising something I said in our previous correspondence — that I'd been living a rather "monkish existence" since she'd taken herself back to Queensland. At first I'd tried to respond to her hand-written letter in kind, but since — as she explained in an unassailably upbeat tone — she was having a baby with another man, everything I wanted to say seemed pointless, impertinent. So I expressed it the only way I could at the time (pathetic, I know) and sent her *The Monk's Rosary*:

1. De Profundis (Nova Schola Gregoriana)
2. The Air that I Breathe (K. D. Lang)
3. Midnight Rain (Paul Kelly)
4. Reckless (Don't be so . . .) (Australian Crawl)
5. No Aphrodisiac (The Whitlams)
6. Brompton Oratory (Nick Cave and the Bad Seeds)
7. Babylon (David Gray)
8. Lover, You Should've Come Over (Jeff Buckley)
9. Razor's Edge (Goanna)
10. Bird on the Wire (Leonard Cohen)
11. If You Wear That Velvet Dress (U2)
12. No Pussy Blues (Grinderman)
13. Waiting for that Day (George Michael)
14. I'm Your Man (Leonard Cohen)

15. Contemplation Rose (Van Morrison)
16. I Dream of Spring (K. D. Lang)
17. Moonlight (Bob Dylan)
18. Vide Cor Meum (Bruno Lazzaretti)
19. Girl from the North Country (Bob Dylan)

Today — more than five years later — I receive a little card: "Tonight I am thinking of you, listening to 'The Monk's Rosary'..."

>leafless
>fingers of the frangipani
>soft spring rain

black
satin
night   alabaster moon
gown
gaping

the sun-bleached rib of a waning moon

Touched
(Sympathy for the Eighth Henry)

And he saw that he had not won out against him and he touched his hip-socket . . .

— Genesis 32:25

As I write these words I can feel that familiar niggling that has dogged me for more than two decades now. In this degree I no longer think of it as pain but a gentle earnest reminder — in the early years it would ambush me . . .. In time I've come to accept it — to live with it just as one learns to live with a sibling or a spouse — and consider it a gift even, bestowing particular sympathies and limitations.

> green eyes
> the cat's face
> never smiles

In 1527, Henry VIII injured his left foot playing tennis, and in the same year was laid up with what has been described as his *"sorre legge"*, the first record of a wound, thought to be an ulcer on his thigh, that would trouble him for the rest of his life. Henry had more than an academic interest in medicine it seems, and being well informed for his day, would have understood better than most exactly where the frontiers of medical science lay. But more than that he knew in his own flesh and bone the dreadful limit of the physician's powers.

> beholden to the illegible stone blue sky

Henry was not inclined to show weakness, it seems, and even made law the Treason Act, forbidding anyone from predicting or speaking of the king's death, which no doubt made it difficult for his physicians to be candid with him. So it is a rare disclosure of vulnerability when he wrote to the Duke of Norfolk excusing himself from travel and confessing: "to be frank with you, which you must keep to yourself, a humour has fallen into our legs and our physicians advise us not to go far in the heat of the day."

>nonsuch palace
>a falcon hugs the unseen
>body of wind

I will never know the inner experience of Henry on his sickbed. At such limits no doubt even kings may be brought to their knees by a nameless foe . . . Mere mortals in the grip of intense pains and agonies can be disposed to dreadful superstitions. But then, a cat may look on a king, and wonder at the exceptional subjectivity of a man that presumed for a time (or was perhaps chosen) to mediate between heaven and earth.

>*Thine is the kingdom . . .*[1]
>the invisible arches
>spotted doves trace

---

1. It strikes me as (perhaps) significant that Henry mandated for inclusion in the Pater Noster this addition to the Lord's Prayer known as "The Doxology" while he was still in communion with the Catholic Church; but that later, after he had broken with Rome (1541), he removed it again by issuing an official edict: "His Grace perceiving now the great diversity of the translations hath caused an uniform translation of the said Pater Noster, Ave, Creed, etc., to be set forth willing all his loving subjects to learn and use the same and straitly (*sic*) commanding all parsons, vicars and curates to read and teach the same to their parishioners."

out of the blue of a broken bird's egg moon

Just a Hunch

> *For Quasimodo ... the cathedral had been successively "egg, nest, house, country, universe."*
>
> — Gaston Bachelard, from 'Nests' in *The Poetics of Space*

Something about the shape of the moon hovering above the shopfront parapets, I think, waiting for the lights at the top of Harthill-Law. — That combined with the thought of where I was headed perhaps, — the Rectory. An image of the church belfry etched in my mind, like an after-image, a distant mountain peak above the haze. Composing in my head on the way. I'd told the Rector previously, the providential significance I attributed to my kyphosis, my 'thorn in the flesh.' Even so, I was still a little surprised at the image that came to me. Before work next morning I Googled "Quasimodo" and "The Hunchback of Notre-Dame".

My (own) hunch had made me curious to read it. I'd taken it from my maternal grandfather's library many years ago — after he died — as a keepsake — that and the old world-globe from his desk. And though I've taken it from my shelf several times in the intervening years, and turned it over, and weighed it in my hand, like a piece of fruit or a finely-crafted blade, for some reason it has as many times been returned, unread, to its place.

According to Wikipedia Hugo chose it as the setting of his story to focus attention on the dilapidation into which the great gothic cathedral had fallen. I followed a link to "Notre-dame Cathedral". The sidebar had a picture with the caption: "16 April 2019. Notre-dame is Burning". I looked at the date: Today!? Thought: Must be a typo . . .

    haunting the belfry
    the ghost of a hunchback
    day moon

dream fading the edge of an ember moon

Too Hard Basket

Are you my son . . . ?

— Genesis 27:24

Compared to Sydney, Sussex Inlet's a sleepy place. Kids would be bored here. There's hardly anyone around, although we're not exactly in the centre of town. The car park is empty except for a mini-bus and one other vehicle, but there are no spaces with shade. My sister and my father get some things out of the back — a present, a birthday cake — as my daughter and I begin making our way up the path to the entrance.

> 'Inasmuch'[1]
> coming to ourselves
> in the mirror-glass doors

We buzz, and after a while the doors open. We make our way down an enclosed corridor that leads to a nurses' station overlooking a spacious common room with lounges and a TV. Various residents are 'parked' or sit in varying states of indignity. Only one seems to be watching the David Attenborough documentary showing on the high-mounted flat-screen. Most are downcast, in differing degrees. Strange — that so many stories, so many lives, should end here. Despite their apparent differences this institution constitutes a simple category — and into this category we have put our grandmother, our mother, our great-grandmother.

---

1. The name of the nursing home is a reference to the King James translation of a parable in The Gospel of Matthew, chapter 25: 31-46.

One of the staff ushers us through to a large dining hall and points her out — sitting with a small group of ladies that don't seem to be talking or interacting, just staring. There's an empty cup of tea on the table in front of her. She watches us impassively as we approach, but seems surprised when she realises we are greeting *her*: "Happy Birthday Grandma," my sister says boisterously. But reposes again when the small bird-like woman beside her becomes suddenly animated with delight, exclaiming, "It's my birthday."

We're jovial, upbeat, a breath of fresh air. We kiss her on her soft flabby cheek, and hug her; she smiles vaguely at no-one in particular. We sit and ask her things, making conversation, trying to remind her; she answers like she always used to — as if speaking to children.

> her wrinkled hand
> smoothing, smoothing
> the table linen
> old habits
> dying hard

Minotaur

... and Jacob's hip was wrenched as he wrestled with him.
— Genesis 32:25

"Do you remember that time we wrestled," he said, "... that place down near the river — where you hire the boats?"

"Audley," I said.

I remembered it vividly; for me it held a secret. But now — in his eighties — this first hint that the occasion was also significant for him. I'd exerted every ounce of strength I could summon in an effort to show him, to warn him. It was not enough. Many years later, on his 65th birthday (I think) our powers had been matched again, that time — mentally . . . Neither would concede defeat. What wounded me most — though no-one stepped in to adjudicate — was that *I* knew *he* knew he was right. I was bluffing, and feared it showed on my face or that some lack of conviction in my voice betrayed me. Another time I remember being strangely disturbed at the sight of him, lying on his back in the dust, beaten, heaving great wheezing sighs of despair or exasperation — the rogue bull we'd spent the afternoon trying to corral trotting off again, tossing its head defiantly, having charged the gate-rail my father was trying to secure. I was supposed to bring it back round again. But in the dying light I stood there, stunned at the sight of him: he seemed to be weeping, although I couldn't say for sure. The next day he got his rifle and took me with him. I watched over his shoulder, amazed how many bullets it took to put it down, and remember feeling a strange kind of pity for the beast . . . A few years ago, when life in its implacable way had brought me too to my knees, I turned to him... for strength but found instead an age-enfeebled man, though still, tragically, unrepentant. — "Yes, I remember."

"I never wrestled you again after that; that was when I knew..."

> white sails
> the rubble-footed prow
> the land shows the sea

river tide

out

in-

to the sea

Again

When the bow is in the clouds, I will see it and remember...
— Genesis 9:16

(26/8/07) This evening at sundown I went walking again. Such a beautiful time — this time of year — when day is turning into night. I went the same way you and I went the night before, across Tasker Park to the river, and around past the electrical tower to the walking bridge. Stopped again on the bridge, and let myself be drawn out, taking it in: the coolness of the evening, the sound of traffic in the distance, the reflections of the trees — the arch of the railway bridge — on the glossy water. Watching litter slipping silently by on the incoming tide. I thought of our walk last evening, of our conversation: I'd made some comment about how beautiful it was, and you agreed, saying how peaceful it was, how — away from the noise — you notice more the sounds of birds, and closer things. Nature did indeed sound closer than the sound of traffic in the distance and the voices of a few kids lingering on the playing fields. The river has a subtle life the city ignores; — that silently glides by, silently breathes . . .

But it's not only the river — the light. The radiant afterglow of that big sky above, the backdrop of silhouettes of palms and pines and rooftops, and the feeling of space on the wide playing fields. Its beauty is overwhelming sometimes. And to be with you in that moment . . .

"— I also love good company and conversation," I said, "but it has to be very good to interrupt something like this . . ."

"— Like the conversations you have with me," you said, beside me on the bridge.

"The reflections are beautiful."

"What reflections?" you asked.

"The arches . . . the trees . . . the moon."

"What are arches?"

"Those half-circle shapes under the railway bridge."

"Like rainbows?"

"Yes, exactly. Like rainbows."

>the sound of rain
>after rain
>rain birds

after the fireworks silence the stars

Beatrice

"What troubles you . . . ?"

— Genesis 21:17

Just before take-off I check my phone. An email from my daughter's mother. I read it quickly. Beginning with strange elation — an almost poetic description of her soul-state during last night's New Year's Eve celebrations — it suddenly descends . . .

> Angkor Wat bas-reliefs
> our guide points out the hells
> have more detail

after the tourist bus
ripples a roadside banana's
tattered leaves

Khmer Rouge

*. . . you are dust,
and to dust you shall return.*

— Genesis 3:19

April 17th 1975 was my 8th birthday. At the time I had no idea it was also day one, year zero in the calendar of the Pol Pot regime.

       tuk tuk dust ground between teeth

Forty years later, I move through the stations of the Killing Fields with my ten-year-old daughter. We have audio-tour headphones on but keep eye-contact with one another: she — making sure we're synchronised; me — watching her reactions to what she's hearing. It's hot. Visitors wander about with their headphones like sleepwalkers distractedly seeking pieces of shade. A joke I heard at school when I was about my daughter's age comes back to me: What's black and runs 100 miles an hour? — A Kampuchean with a food voucher. At the time I thought Kampuchea was in Africa. I pictured a small black boy with a big head on a skinny body tearing down a dirt track waving his voucher. For some reason it made me giggle. I told it myself on several occasions. It was easy to remember. I don't recall anyone saying it wasn't really funny.

       out of town the skin colour of earth

The Mouths of Babes

. . . and he gave her the child, and sent her away . . .
— Genesis 21:14

Her voice sounds young, tom-boyish, good-natured — confident. She's turned out alright.

The interviewer asks what it was like for her, before coming to Australia.

My father left when I was real young. I think he was in the military or something. It was just my mother and my two younger brothers. My mother told me once how she'd seen lots of people being shot, lots of dead bodies and stuff. I think she's still traumatised by that when she thinks about it. But I don't remember anything like that. I just remember travelling around in the backs of trucks mostly. And being hungry. Yeah, we didn't have any food so my mother would breastfeed me even though I was like seven . . .

Just then the Blue Tooth interrupts, my ring tone kicks in — a client about a job. When the call ends the program comes back on but I've missed quite a bit.

. . . I don't want to sound racist or anything, but when I got to Australia I'd never seen so many white people. It was scary . . .

> check out queue
> a young mother
> tries her other card

morning sun
a little skink
in a crevice of the bricks

Thing-in-itself

... I hid myself ...

— Genesis 3:10

His little face was there in a big window of the childcare centre, peering down over the sill at the outside world. I waved as I drove into the car park, though probably he couldn't see me through reflections in my windscreen. His impassive face like a flower followed my car, stopping where it stopped. Parked, I wound down my window and noticing he was looking, waved again. For a split second I thought I discerned an almost imperceptible retraction in that little being and instinctively looked away, not wanting to shatter, as it were, the 'fourth wall' of one not yet ready to be seen.

>tarnishing reflections
>on a reed-sheltered pond
>autumn zephyr

fungal society
the year's last
outing

Big Bend

>unhooking a sooty grunter crumbed in river sand

Only now (looking at this photo my sister has sent me) do I notice the long shadows and warm crimson-orange hues of the early morning sun on the bank of the Burdekin . . .

>unzipping stars deep in the night river

I woke, needing to take a leak. The moon had set, everyone sleeping soundly in their tents, the campfire settled to a warm nest. The river soundlessly slipping by in its endless way. I felt a faint yearning — lifting my eyes from the calm mirror to those ancient constellations . . . but was called back before long by the close song of crickets . . . to our humble camp, and became aware of a presence — like, and yet not like, that of a person: a large melaleuca growing more or less parallel with the flow of the river. This same paperbark, I now realised, had, during the last flood, collected our firewood. We'd been tugging those sun-bleached tufts and driftwood from its branches. It'd been forced to bow before the power of an engorged brown god, prostrate, though not entirely uprooted. It still grew, but now in a manner more befitting the terrible mercy of the one on whom its life depended. Under the wing of this prone tree our little camp nestled like a child.

I remember looking up at the stars again, drawing a deep breath, then burrowing back into my tent.

>aurora sky
>the drift of the bob-float
>through a veil of mist

winter wind
a pair of sneakers dangle
from the wire

Acrobat

. . . and they became one flesh.

— Genesis 2:24

That's one of the bad things about having parents that are divorced, she says.

What? I ask.

You have to do twice as much grocery shopping, she laughs. — I was here yesterday with Mum.

Yeah, I smile. That would be a bummer.

It's school holidays. She's spent the day at the Botanic Gardens with her Nan while I was working.

At lunchtime I got a text from Mum's phone:

Hi Dad I wrote a haiku for you:

the spider's shining tight-rope held I wonder about my chances

> Sunday drop-off
> the distance between us
> she walks alone

early traffic
on the peaks of the city
touches of sunlight

in the time it takes him
to answer the door
thistledown

Nomenclator

> *. . . and whatever the human called a living creature, that was its name.*
>
> —Genesis 2:19

Nominal aphasia, a psychologist once told me, describing symptoms of early onset dementia. In my father's case it was not so much a capacity he was losing as one he never fully acquired.

Now that we're old enough we tease him about his 'thing language'. Back then we had to compensate.

Can one of youse kids get me that thing on the side of the . . . what's-it-called . . . the flat thing . . .

Which thing? I'd ask.

You know the thing I mean, he'd bark back, as if I were being smart with him.

And so I went—in search of nameless things.

> evening train
> waking to the strange
> word on my lips

tyre swing
the last of the sun's light
in the old pepper tree

Butterfly Net

> morning breeze
> trembling in the spider's web
> a dandelion seed

I have always loved the great Russian authors. But recently I discovered a great Russian author that writes in English! I finally got around to reading *Speak, Memory* by Vladimir Nabokov during a recent and — it turns out — fortunate bout of influenza. Fate it seems decreed this book would stay with me more than two decades since the day I first found it 'on special' — the sticker still on it says — in one of a regular round of bookshops in Brisbane I used to trawl as a young university student. Since then it had been cycled from bookshelf to box and back again — unread — through at least a dozen rental houses. Yet there it still was: a strange specimen, as it were, in my collection. The book itself is a Penguin paperback edition. On the front, in pale peppermint relief, is a sepia photograph of the young Caucasian author smoking, looking alert but very much at ease in the prow of a rowboat adrift at Cambridge during the Spring of 1920. Some reference another writer made to Nabokov moved me to find it out and settle down at last to reading.

> butterfly farm
> the wanderer throwing itself
> against the net

Today I find myself diverted by a little cameo, an unlikely specimen, from a chapter which recalls the Nabokov family holidays to *Biarritz* — a place which, since hitherto I never knew existed, Nabokov has created virtually *ex nihilo* for my solitary good pleasure. Why has this odd passing character remained with me after reading? Why did he remain with Nabokov so perfectly preserved for thirty-something years then to be suddenly brought back to life? It occurs to me that these textual recollections of "the palpitating *plage*" by the forty-something-year-old man were first captured by a ten-year-old boy rarely seen without his butterfly net. Amidst all the "movement and sound" on the beach Nabokov recalls those "provided by venders hawking *cacahuètes*, sugared violets, pistachio ice cream of a heavenly green, cachou pellets, and huge convex pieces of dry, gritty, waferlike stuff that came from a red barrel." And among all these distracting delicacies he makes particular mention of "the waffleman", whose uncouth manner is remembered with a curious sympathy, and whose fortunes his gaze seems to have followed on its erratic way up and down the beach. When called, he would bring his red barrel and plant it "Pisa-like" in the sand before his customers, presumably so they could judge for themselves the honesty with which he spun the "arrow-and-dial arrangement with numbers on the lid". (*Biarritz* — although Nabokov mentions this only incidentally as "absolutely out of bounds" — had a casino.) He remembers the rasping and whirring sound the spinning arrow made before it stopped: "Luck," he explains, "was supposed to fix the size of a sou's worth of wafer." And then concludes, "The bigger the piece, the more I was sorry for him." The writer's relation to life — the thought occurs to me — is not unlike the boy monarch — in early modern Europe — to the whipping boy appointed to accompany him.

    still struggling
    the tiger moth's wing dust
    blackens the web

tears in the web
a moth enters
its second cocoon

Darwin

In the beginning...

— Genesis 1:1

He began on May 31st 1876 at the request of a German editor and for his own amusement and the possible interest of his children and grandchildren to write an account of "the development of my mind and character." This was six years before he died. He writes, he says, "as if I were a dead man in another world looking back at my own life."

Seven years before that, in a letter to a friend, he had said, "If I had twenty more years and was able to work, how I should have to modify the *Origin*, and how much the views on all points will have to be modified! Well it is a beginning, and that is something...."

Under a section titled "Religious Belief" he asserts, we must not "overlook the probability of the constant inculcation in a belief in God on the minds of children producing so strong and perhaps an inherited effect on their brains not yet fully developed, that it would be as difficult for them to throw off their belief in God, as for a monkey to throw off its instinctive fear and hatred of a snake." And yet he concedes that "I cannot pretend to throw the least light on such abstruse problems. The mystery of the beginning of all things is insoluble by us..."

> a plover's cry
> following the course
> of the night river

In the final pages, speaking as a man in at least one sense dead to himself, he says, "I am not conscious of any change in my mind during the last thirty years, excepting in one point presently to be mentioned." It is evident, both from the letter quoted earlier, and in the final passage from which I draw all subsequent citations, that when he speaks of a change in his mind he is not referring to an opinion or theory, but to the *disposition* of his mind. For in various places he speaks about the great "pleasure" and "delight" he once took in poetry, visual art and music up to and even beyond the age of thirty, but notes that "now for many years" he cannot "endure" to read a line of poetry, that Shakespeare "nauseate[s]" him, that he had "lost any taste for pictures or music", and that even fine scenery "does not cause me the exquisite delight which it formerly did". "My mind," he laments, "seems to have become a kind of machine for grinding general laws out of large collections of facts, but why this should have caused the atrophy of that part of the brain alone, on which the higher tastes depend, I cannot conceive." It is with rueful candour he tells the living, "[I]f I had to live my life again I would have made a rule to read some poetry and listen to some music at least once every week" — admitting that the "loss of these tastes is a loss of happiness, and may possibly be injurious to the intellect, and more probably to the moral character, by enfeebling the emotional part of our nature." Who can say what might have been? In this subjunctive mood I am unsure how to read the man who in one breath rues the atrophication of his higher aesthetic tastes and blesses all novelists whose "works of the imagination," he says, "though not of a very high order, have been for years a wonderful relief and pleasure to me." And he is quite particular on this point: he likes, he says, all novels "if moderately good, and if they don't end unhappily — against which a law ought to be passed." I wonder if we are to take this final word in jest: "A novel, according to my taste, does not come into the first class unless it contains some person whom one can thoroughly love, and if it be a pretty woman all the better."[1]

    after the rain
    the gully remembers
    a currawong song

---

[1]. All quotations are from *The Autobiography of Charles Darwin 1808 – 1882* (Ed. by Nora Barlow) Norton 2005.

Water

> *And Isaac dug anew the wells of water that had been dug in the days of Abraham his father . . .*
> — Genesis 26:18

In a way it's a privilege (my thoughts diverted by a discarded plastic bottle I notice in the scrub beside the track) — that I can remember a time before plastic bottles; can appreciate the primitive possibilities of such a useful thing beyond its commercially ordained role as a one-off delivery device. *Dispose of thoughtfully,* it reads. That a thoughtful person might consider the possibility of not disposing of it at all . . . the possibilities of keeping it . . . of reusing or at least recycling it . . . or not buying into such philistine commodification in the first place. But such seem not to have occurred to the marketeer that coughed up that symptomatic sentence, — let alone the one that flung it there. — Symptomatic, yes, or cynical. A privilege — that I still have some memory, some sense of what our race once called 'need'.

> lenten moon
> the ribbed wake
> of a moorhen

rain-flecks on the windscreen
between city skyscrapers
a gull

Ubirr

And the Lord God made skin coats for the human and his woman, and he clothed them.

— Genesis 3:21

The shady overhangs and crevices of the rocky outcrops at the edge of the Nadab floodplain shelter an abundance of aboriginal rock art. Many beings are depicted here, including Mimi spirits, the first Dreamtime ancestors. But animal paintings predominate. Initially the decorative intricacy and stylistic patterning are most striking. The information posts and my Kakadu National Park booklet refer to it as "X-ray art", and not without reason. It's not what I'd call scientific illustration exactly, but the more one looks the more one is impressed by the remarkable display of anatomical structure—anatomies of the animals by which traditional human inhabitants of the area apparently subsisted.

Climbing higher, the vista of the floodplain extends out to the horizon. There are six seasons here. Now is the end of Gurrung, the hot dry season. I sit a while in a little piece of shade imagining the great expanse during Gudjewg, covered in water. Or the vast sky during Banggerreng, the "knock 'em down storm season".

On the way down I pass again a striking painting of a long-necked turtle and another of a Barramundi; but the more I contemplate the more inappropriate the term "X-ray art" seems, promoting as much ignorance as it does understanding of the way such intimate knowledge of our animal brethren was no doubt obtained. Among them, too, an odd one: the form of a man, but conspicuously opaque, like a silhouette, standing, hands in pockets, sporting what seems to be a pipe.

> security screen
> the official asks if it's
> a harmonica

overcast the corresponding river dove coos

Mrs Darwin

> *And the human called names to all the cattle and to the fowl of the heavens and to all the beasts of the field, but for the human no sustainer beside him was found.*
>
> — Genesis 2:20

Mrs Darwin was concerned about side-effects that her husband's scientific work seemed to be having on the subject — Charles himself, that is — "my own dear Nigger" as she affectionately addresses him in a personal letter.

> balcony view
> a slow crack of thunder
> spreads through the firmament

I have been reading the complete Nora Barlow edition of *The Autobiography of Charles Darwin* given me recently by my wife. Having finished the *AB* proper and skimmed through some of the Appendices and Notes I come across two of Mrs Darwin's letters to Charles in a section titled "Mrs Darwin's papers on Religion" (Note Five). In these her solicitude for his spiritual life is tenderly and delicately expressed. The first, though undated, was written "on a sheet of old-fashioned note-paper" shortly after their marriage on January 29, 1839. We know this because Charles tells us in the *AB*. Addressing his children there he speaks of their mother affectionately, with deep gratitude and adoration. The tenderness and reverence with which he honours her is hard to convey. For example: "I marvel at my good fortune that she, so infinitely my superior in every single moral quality, consented to be my wife." Or:

"She has been my greatest blessing, and I can declare that in my whole life I have never heard her utter one word which I had rather have been unsaid." At the end of this remarkable passage he inserted a brief note in parentheses: "(Mem: her beautiful letter to myself preserved, shortly after our marriage.)" This letter which was found among Emma's papers after her death has a small annotation at the end that Charles himself had written:

> "When I am dead, know
> that many times, I
> have kissed and cried
> over this. C. D."

The second letter was written in or before 1861 which we know from another notation that Charles wrote at the bottom of it: "God Bless you C. D. 1861." The letter itself indicates that it was written during one of his many periods of illness. Like the first — though it was written more than twenty years earlier — it is solicitous of his spiritual life, but she is so delicate in her manner of expressing this. It is only that she confesses "I feel presumptuous in writing this to you" that alerts me to what she is so tenderly intimating: the aetiology of his recurrent illnesses. The fifth supplementary note to the Nora Barlow edition, "On Charles Darwin's Ill-health", begins with these words: "Health anxieties haunt the pages of the *Autobiography*, yet Charles Darwin's many medical advisers never reached definite conclusions as to the cause of his long bouts of illness. No diagnosis was ever made of a causal organic disorder." Keeping one finger in the notes I flip back to two paragraphs near the end of the *AB* which begin, "I have said that in one respect my mind has changed during the last twenty or thirty years." In these paragraphs he describes his "curious and lamentable loss" of what he calls "the higher aesthetic tastes". But I notice here the following sentence which on second reading seems to have an almost confessional tone: "A man with a mind more highly organised or better constituted than mine, would not I suppose have thus suffered . . .." I wonder if this was a discreet admission, perhaps the payment of a debt he felt he owed Emma? And if one were to make a small change to the wording of another sentence: "[An autobiography — or even better — a Life], according to my taste, does not come into the first class unless it contains some person whom one can thoroughly love, and if it be a pretty woman all the better."

Just before I turn in I glance at the last section before the index:

"NOTE SIX
Page and line references to the more important previously omitted passages"

> the sound of midnight
> rain gives way
> to crickets

river reeds
a dragonfly tracks its double
through the morning mist

mangrove mud
an ibis fettered to a single use
plastic bag

Recovery

> "Where are you?"
>
> — Genesis 3:9

From time to time he leans on me . . . to get his balance. Like a man recovering from an injury. Usually just a phone call. Nothing heavy. Needs to run something by me. Check his thinking sounds about right. Suspects people are testing him, or someone may have put something in his water.

> bedside window
> the shadow mottled page
> of Rilke's Archaic Torso

valley sky
the thread of the trail lost
in a sift of rain

Wild Rosemary

And the Lord's messenger found her by a spring of water in the wilderness . . .

— Genesis 16:7

On the 14th instant the deceased, Catherine Foster, was found drowned in the lagoon on the Condobolin Road, but there was no evidence to show how deceased got into the water.[1] That was the verdict the Magistrate returned. The 14th instant? I check the dates in the pamphlet I'm reading and deduce that this strange, precise expression must be an old-fashioned official way of saying the 14th day of the said month, namely, October 1898. I look over at my daughter — about to tell her how Kate Kelly died — and see she's engrossed in a pamphlet about Ben Hall.

> Kate Foster [née Kelly]
> a sprig of wild rosemary
> on her headstone

We're lying in the shade of a large Casuarina. The grass is cool and green. A nearby hose-tap is dripping. I look out across the sections of grave stones. It's hard to believe this morning we were standing among rank wild rosemary and black cypress pine gazing out across the western plains from a rugged granite ridge somewhere in the Goobang National Park.

---

1. This extract and subsequent extracts are from the pamphlet Kate Kelly produced by the Forbes Shire Council with the assistance of the Forbes & District Historical Society, The Kate Kelly Project, and The Kate Kelly Trail.

> Burrabadine Peak
> the knock of our stone
> on the cairn

It is claimed, the pamphlet says, she went under the name of Kate Hennessey or Ada because she did not want it known generally that she was a sister of the Kelly boys. When she came to Forbes she worked as a 'domestic' for a number of local families. People described her as 'a nice looking girl, with long dark hair' and as 'a good servant'. Five months before Kate's body was found, her husband, William Henry Foster, or 'Bricky' as he was known, was charged in the Forbes Magistrate's Court with using abusive language 'in his own house to his wife, within the hearing of the public.' Between 25th November 1888 when she married Bricky, and October 1898 when she died, Kate bore 6 children. The first of which, the pamphlet tactfully states, was born in March of the year following their wedding. Apparently Bricky had regular employment on the Burrawang Station some 50km west of Forbes township but had visited Kate the night before her disappearance and 'remonstrated' with her for being under the influence of drink. The last person known to have seen Kate was her neighbour, Susan Hurley, whom she asked to take care of her baby Catherine, and also to write a note for her, but no records of the contents of this note have survived.

> beyond the epitaph
> spotted doves
> frotting in the gloom

The brochure contains a number of pictures including an illustration of Kate being congratulated by her father after winning the Wagga Cup. But there is one that fascinates me: an old photograph of Kate with Ellen Kelly (her mother) and her family taken in front of the house that Ned built for his mother at Greta in Victoria following Ellen's release from prison in 1881, 7 years before Kate married Bricky, 17 years before she was found dead. Kate is wearing a black dress and hat and a small girl — her youngest sibling Alice whom she helped Ellen give birth to — is clinging to her knee. Kate is looking directly at the camera encouraging Alice to look too. The sun's light is falling obliquely, casting shadows from right to left. Her skeletal resemblance to Ned is accentuated by the contrast of light and shade. Between Ellen and Kate the open doorway reveals a dark interior. I gaze into that darkness but can't make out anything; the grainy flecks in the sepia are like stars in the night sky.

    dirt road slowly lengthening sheep shadows

evening star wobbling in the waterhen's wake

No Man is an Island

... but for the human ...
— Genesis 2:20

This morning I disturbed a grey heron's reverie, walking out along the broken vertebrae of jagged rocks to Barlings Island. It watched a while, how far I'd come. Too close, evidently. Uplifting itself, banking into the breeze, it wafted off around the head, needing a certain distance to be at ease. Heron-like, I stood a while, beneath ashes of a Lenten moon . . . A pair of pied cormorant were fishing around the rocks, alternate heads, appearing, disappearing . . .

> tyre tracks in the sand
> a lobster shell, remains
> of a fire

cold sand satellites upstaging the stars

Shipwreck

    the strange star that hides each night behind another day

Something has shifted, the tide turned. Each time I look up over the salt-blurred rims of my reading glasses, more jagged rocks are uncovered. As if growing from the soft-skinned sand, rugged shoulders rise, wrapped in matted furs of wrack, bedraggled, bladder-beaded rosaries, entangled, broken, strewn about, among — wearing stony expressions like faces forged in the long nightmare of history. Just beyond a crooked line of shivering pools, another scrum of waves packs down, spume-crested, curve-backed, sand-hauling; a great unfathomable mother withdraws.

    a wren on a fence post waves through the dune grass

I'm nestled at the sandy foot of a precipice off Melville Point, reading. This isn't Cape Cod, and I am only holidaying here. But against the many voices and soughing surf and wind I have lashed myself to the mast of Thoreau with unstopped ears. It is a stoic tone in which he describes the scene: the wreckage of the brig *St John*, from Galway — laden as it had been with migrants (fleeing, I gather, the great potato famine, since the year, he tells us, was 1849): the sight of the rough wooden boxes on the beach and the people of Cohasset coming and going, dealing with "the business". In an age of aeronautics and GPS technology, such vivid episodes would be lost in Lethean depths were it not for shipwrights like Thoreau: a vessel like *Cape Cod* can bear one back across oceans of time: the "many marble feet" he witnessed, or "the coiled-up wreck of a human hulk, gashed by the rocks or fishes . . . with wide-open and staring eyes, yet lustreless, dead-lights." "Sometimes there were two or more children, or a parent and a child, in the same box, and on the lid would perhaps be written with red chalk, 'Bridget such-a-one, and sister's child.'" — The full significance of this red inscription he discovered afterward: "I have since heard . . . that a woman who had come over before, but had left her infant behind for her sister to bring, came and saw in one [coffin], — probably the one whose superscription I have quoted, — her child in her sister's arms, as if the sister had meant to be found thus; and within three days after, the mother died from the effect of that sight."[1]

From this woman's grief I look up again: A lone gull — cruciform, wind-buoyed, head hung, — wings a low wafty way above the spray, beneath the sun.

> headland monument
> the fields this rust-scabbed
> anchor ploughed

---

1. From the chapter, 'The Shipwreck' in *Cape Cod*, by Henry David Thoreau.

her little hand in mine
another sweep
of the lighthouse beam

Ariadne

God called the dry land Earth, and the waters that were gathered together he called Seas.

— Genesis 1:10

...amor fati: *that one wants nothing to be other than it is, not in the future, not in the past, not in all eternity.*

— Nietzsche, *Ecce Homo*

I saw him really for the first time through her eyes — reliving holiday impressions, holding them up like negatives to a thin-curtained window of light. She came to mind, and without really meaning to I followed the trace of her through convoluted passage ways, taken back to a moment when, as if moved by an overwhelming affection, she rose from a rock behind him, where she'd been watching dreamily, drew close, and slipping her arms about his waist, placed her chin on his shoulder and for a moment they looked out together, toward the same horizon. Something in that seemed beautiful. Something . . . like a mother whispering into the dreams of her sleeping child . . .

"The love I feel for you this moment I cannot withhold; it belongs to you as much as me."

> cloud drift
> the rubble-footed prow
> the land shows the sea

What she loves: when I saw it, it also seemed beautiful to me: the fisherman in his element, the heavy bodied ocean heaving, rising, lunging at the podium. If the force of its battery moved that rock it was imperceptible to me — or the fisherman standing on it, relaxed, attuned, patient in expectancy, with the relentless sea snorting and fuming at his feet. How unperturbed he seemed, how sure at the elemental limit of its reach, with rod and reel, and the fine neural line between: his barbed hook feeling for some sudden promise in the deep, yielding flesh; a barnacle on the rocky carapace — segmented with veins and blades of tempered iron, pocked with perfectly transparent pools.

Although it is not completely true to say — the blazing sun goes down for the day, at the interface all elements behave as they do.

> headland
> a distant sail on the brink
> of an otherworld

dune grass
a pair of thongs waiting
for their feet

My Brother's Keeper

. . . let us bake bricks . . . lest we be scattered . . .
— Genesis 11:3, 4

> falling star
> little by little
> his wormwood

I stay silent, listening. He's sensitive, like a roebuck. Tone and timing are crucial. Though he speaks of things — a past — to which I too could lay claim, one whiff of insubordination to the tyranny of his narrative and — he's gone.

> out of the mist
> a muzzle
> dawn doe

False beliefs, false suppositions, false memories . . . the footings of identity, baked bricks in the tower of fear, spiked with a perversity of weapons. The narrative ossifies, becomes harder to unbelieve. So much has been invested in the lie. Beyond a point truth has the aspect of death.

> electrical storm
> coloured wires woven
> into the nest

a
rain
drop
glissando
release of
a leaf

Family Business

> "... If you take the left hand, then I shall go right; and if you take the right hand, I shall go left..."
>
> — Genesis 13:9

After texting my clients and my brother to tell them I'd come down with the flu and wouldn't be able to make it to work, I took some paracetamol, put my phone on silent, and went back to bed. When I woke again, everyone had left the house which by then had been warmed by the winter sun. But my body was aching. Thinking perhaps some fresh air and sunshine would help I dressed and went out for a walk. Meandering along my usual track beside the polluted creek I made my way to the seat — a rough-squared block of chisel-marked stone — I'd placed previously in a sunny spot near a large fig tree under which lately I've been spending some time. It's not quite like other figs I've known; it seems to have more branches which rise and separate right from the level of the ground, as if each branch were a separate — yet grown-together — trunk. It is perhaps the most striking and luxuriant of trees in the vicinity with its wide spreading branches, some bowing all the way to the ground.

> winter sun
> the boy in me still dreams
> a way up the tree

In a way it's beautiful, and yet — apart from the little brown warblers that sometimes rummage among its roots and debris — birds rarely visit its branches. It seems deserted, lonely. The only company within the overbearing expanse of its canopy is the large broken trunk of a dead banksia. As I raised and mobilized my sun-warmed — though still aching — bones, readying myself for the walk home, I paused at the carcass of the old banksia laying my hands on its warty, nobbled bark.

>urban developments
>mansions higher
>than the steeple

dam building
we watch the stream
make another way

cold comfort
the smell of water
in the stone

Uluru

> *... Abraham raised his eyes and saw the place from afar*
> —Genesis 22:4

They say it makes the heart grow fonder ...

A little girl about your age is staring. Behind me the sun is setting. I'm watching The Rock (that I've decided not to climb) out the opened back of my camper. She's still just standing there, a few meters in front of me, strawberry-blonde hair and tiny blue beady-wide eyes. I'm lying back on one elbow, sipping a cup of tea, journal open on the mattress beside me. I smile. You're looking the wrong way, I say, pointing to the blazing rock behind her in the distance. She seems not to comprehend, mumbles something I can hardly hear, and moves away to the side, not taking her eyes off me. The sun has set. The deep rippled Rock turns dusty-mauvey-crimson, like a hot coal fallen, cooling in the sand. When I look again she's playing in the dirt, talking to herself or some invisible friend, heaping a little ochre-red mound. Its surface, now, like hairless skin — ancient, wrinkled, baggy — of some prehistoric elephant, mired, half sunk in quicksand. Look Mummy, she says, her little fingers marching up the pile: Climbing the Rock.

> dark emu
> the shape of your absence
> in the stars

still warm
long after sundown
gravestone

Bethel

... he took the stone that he had put under his head and set it up for a pillar ...

— Genesis 28:18

Today I serviced an elderly widow's toilet and taps. She made me instant coffee served with plain Arnott's biscuits. I made conversation. In broken English she told me how she and her husband had come from Sicily to Sydney, to give the children a better life. Her daughter is married now, living in Queensland; her son, somewhere in Germany. Over the years the neighbourhood has changed so much, she no longer knows anyone in the street: No-one cares, she said, voice quavering.

> abandoned quarry
> the fig tree silently
> splitting a rock

Afterwards I ate my lunch in the shade of a large palm tree in the grounds of a nearby church. Despite signs of dilapidation — the toppled gravestones and the root-buckled paths — there was evidence of care: the inviting lawns seemed well kept. The old stone church had withstood the test of time. Leaving I paused a moment where two paths criss-crossing the grounds intersect in front of the entrance to the church: the worn-down old stone steps and doorsill remain.

> giving moss
> a place to gather
> gully stones

living long enough to feel the need for stone

The Great Ocean Road

beholden to the illegible stone blue sky

It may be superstition or presumption to see in events or their timing portentous significances. And yet some happenings, depending in what light one reads them, do seem to bear within themselves certain symbolic aptitudes. So at least it seems to me now reflecting on the coincidence of one such event with a kind of pilgrimage I once took along The Great Ocean Road.

That meandering, scenic, soul-opening drive around the southern Victorian coast of Australia features a number of spectacular limestone and sandstone rock-formations that are, given our Christian and colonial heritage, tellingly named The Twelve Apostles (though only eight still stand) and The London Bridge.

I visited these on the 14th of January 1990 during the summer holidays of my second year in training for the ministry. On the 16th of January I heard a report on the radio that The London Bridge had (the previous day) unexpectedly collapsed leaving two souls separated from the mainland on the remnant salt-encrusted pillar. . . .

Standing out here, 24 years later, in my little suburban backyard, on this chilly winter night looking up at the same stars Abraham beheld, dimmed though they be by the glare of the city's lights, and making out still those ancient constellations, I wonder what those two hallowed souls made of it at the time, and after-times. . . .. It has certainly caused me to think — being one of the last people ever to walk out across that ancient arch — as if immune to the erosive, corrosive forces of time . . .

    deep rust where the analogy begins

Letter from a Blacksmith

Zillah . . . bore Tubal-cain, who forged every tool of copper and iron.

— Genesis 4:22

The contrast with paper could hardly be more stark. What page could pass through fire, let alone a bellows-blasted furnace? Its blued metal tested, transformed in the urge of the artisan: its hardened ram's head, its spiral-twisted horns, fashioned in that liminal glow, a softening extorted by extraordinary heat, wherein was formed this . . . kernel in my fist. Below its head, in the squared shaft, an elegant one-hundred-and-eighty-degree twist, and below that, at the point it begins to round and thin and taper to a shiv, the punched impression of a miniature dragon-head: signature of the blacksmith. It does nothing but gather dust on my bookshelf. A useless tool, made according to things that no longer exist. I weigh it in my hand, admire its rustic craftsmanship, wonder at its metallurgic lineage. When I acquired it years ago, from a blacksmith in Lithgow, the age of hand-written letters was all but dead, already passing out of mind. It has never opened a letter since, or secured a page from the mischievous wind. Its silence a strange quixotic elegy to life's redundant things. Its maker a noble misfit.

>   purr
>   of the postman's bike
>   chastening wind

Pocketknife

> *. . . never more than today has He made His presence felt by "being absent."*
>
> — Thomas Merton, *The Inner Experience*

I found it in the scree beside the walking track at Newnes — on the back-way up to the Glow Worm Tunnel from the strange ruins of the old shale oil colliery. It stayed with me two or three years until it was confiscated by security at Bangkok airport. I forgot it was in the daypack I was carrying. Too late by then. The official said it would be destroyed. But I find it hard to believe — someone could throw something like that into a furnace! Ten years have passed since then but still, from time to time, something reminds me . . . I find myself wondering where it is . . . now . . .

> gilding the curves
> of the railway tracks
> winter sunlight

winter sunshine
twanging dew drops
from the clothesline

warm concrete
green mandarins
among the quivering leaves

To Be or Not To Be

Go from your country and your kindred and your father's house to the land that I will show you.

— Genesis 12:1

... the individual life proceeds in a movement from state to state. Every state is posited by a leap.

— Kierkegaard, *The Concept of Anxiety*

The night before last, in a dream, I was walking over a bridge — then I was in a small aeroplane which lost altitude and had to land — then in a small boat which filled with water and finally sank.

Last night I had somehow gained access to the home of a family I did not know. They returned and discovered me there. Until I woke, the dream held me in a Kafkaesque state of tension, feeling inexplicably suspect and awkward before those good people who remained all the while courteous and hospitable despite my intrusion.

> spring wind
> trying to open the gate
> without breaking the web

summer heat
the odd-shaped package
on her doorstep

streetlight

my undoing

her negligee

of venetian

shadows

Johannes Climacus

"It is not good for the human to be alone..."
— Genesis 2:18

Not far from the house where I live is a track that leads through a little strip of bushland, beside a quiet creek that surprisingly few people frequent. I usually go walking there early in the morning or in the late afternoon, both if I have time. The sense now that I am known to those that dwell there, that I am free to enter and pass through the realm of their society is part of the privilege.

>   bush hermitage three legs from the leaf scroll

Somehow this track has found its way through the bush and became the constant companion of the creek. There are other side tracks: one leading to a rock overhang where a homeless man has been living for years, another less trodden track branches off and turns up a hill. From the top — beyond the scaly skin of terracotta tile rooves covering the prehistoric bodies of suburban hills — one can trace the full circle of horizon interrupted only by a few tall trees.

>   winter sunset of another unsigned masterpiece

Usually inclined — though less of late — to go off the main track, I part the thin curtain of leaves that close again behind me, shrouding the little trail's entrance, and climb the ancient gnarled staircase. Sand-stone and tree-root, scuffed and polished, weathered and washed by those ascending and descending: the wind and feet, sun and cold and rain. In this way not one tread is the same as the last. Two steps cannot be taken the same without stumbling on some unique irregularity. I've climbed these stairs so many times, even on moonless nights, and fancy I know them now by heart. In places the sandstone treads are worn down to raw ochres in slight hollows — by my footsteps too — after those that have gone before, before those that will come . . .. Near the top I recall the lovers of Rilke's ninth elegy: *Threshold: what it means to them, wearing down the ancient doorsill, lightly, a little more*

evening star the sound of a heart beating flat-out on a stone

moonlight I tell her the scent of wattle blossom

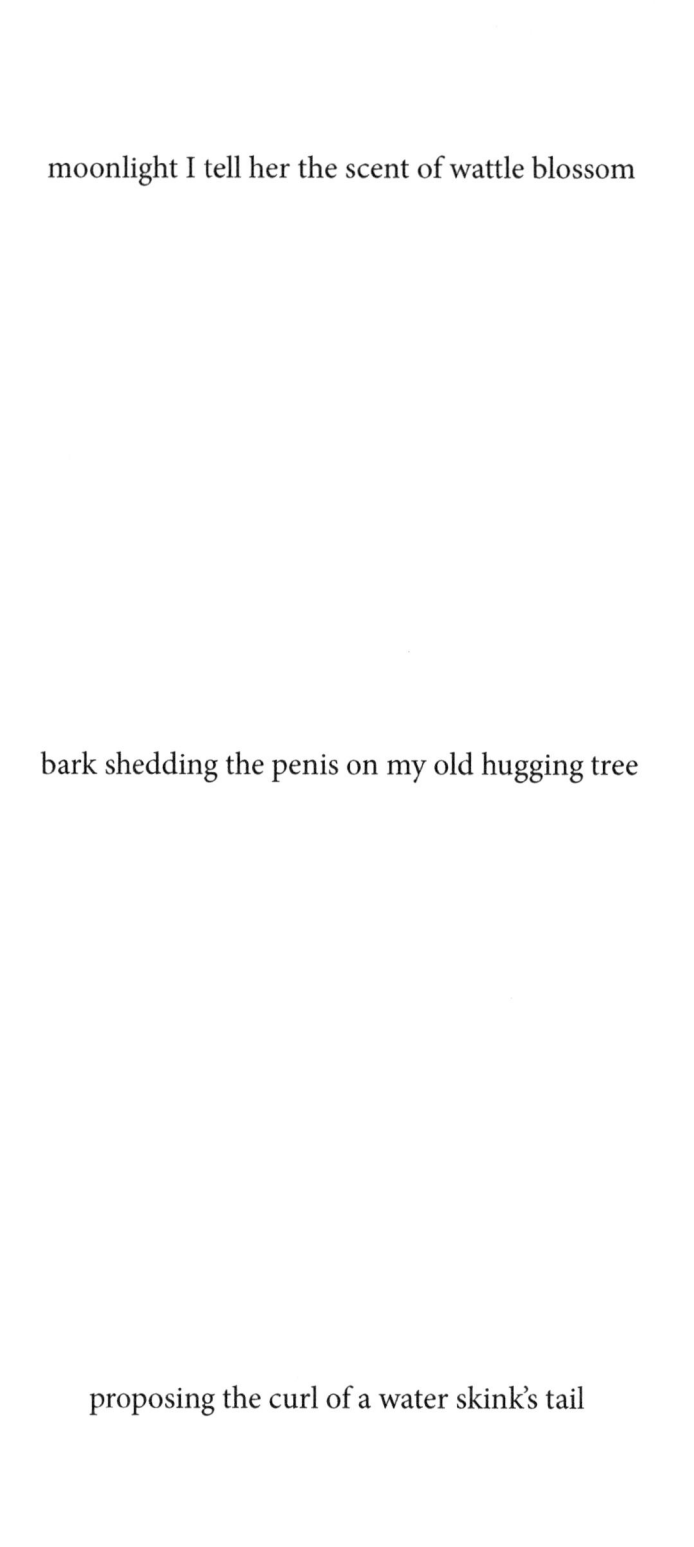

bark shedding the penis on my old hugging tree

proposing the curl of a water skink's tail

The Ring

The covenant is eternity's beginning in time.
— Kierkegaard, 'On the Occasion of a Wedding',
Three Discourses on Imagined Occasions

After dinner we take the path along the south bank. Beside us the river is a dark mirror and beyond the inverted treeline, the depths of its luminous sky. It's almost still — the night. Undistorted by wind. Inner suburbia. Softened in street light. The sun's absence and a little wine have restored equilibrium of the senses. A new ambience is emerging, spacious and intimate: the arterial flow of distant traffic... the cry of a lapwing punctuating the course of the night river... the pulse of crickets... echo of our own footsteps. It's such a little thing. Such a big thing. I feel its shape in my pocket, turning it over and over, and not really knowing how I will begin. But approaching I remember where...

As if expecting us we find the little jetty waiting, there on the edge of the pond, minding our place, as it were. And for the second time, sit together on its decking.

It feels weird, I say, asking a question that's already been answered...

> two turrets
> of a sleeping circus
> deep in the marsh pond

ocean roar
a narrow passage
through the heath

UXO

... at the east of the garden of Eden he placed the cherubim and the flame of the whirling sword ...
— Genesis 3:24

... when we examine a nest, we place ourselves at the origin of confidence in the world, we receive a beginning of confidence, an urge toward cosmic confidence.
— Gaston Bachelard, *The Poetics of Space*

I just wanted her to be the first to know, but my announcement detonates something ...

I always knew you and Mum wouldn't get back together, she says, with a wrenching groan, exploding into convulsive sobs, but now you definitely won't ...

Sitting on the same rock shelf, in the same little cove, looking out toward the same Pacific horizon ... I find myself thinking back to our trip through South East Asia ... her wandering happily among bomb craters at the Plain of Jars, near Phonsavan in Laos ... I should have known, nothing could ever be the same after that ...

Her sobbing subsides. She sits up and stares silently into the offing.

At school we do this thing called Smiling Mind — a meditation app. There's this one called The Wishing Tree. I hope you're not mad at me for this, but whenever we do the wishing tree I always wish ... you and Mum ...

    fallen nest all that was woven into this

flotsam shore how it all came to this

	outgoing tide
	the little portion
	a shell retains

Bar Island
(on our honeymoon)

> *And the eyes of two were opened, and they knew they were naked, and they sewed fig leaves . . .*
>
> — Genesis 2:25

We're standing near the top looking down through a window in the tangled bush to the grid of oyster farms in Broken Bay. Here — where Berowra creek meets the greater Hawkesbury, today at least — is a peaceful place. The Ancients would say a halcyon day. A tantalizing breeze carries a faint scent of blossom up through the trees. I'm trying to place it . . . What? she says coming up behind, slipping her arms around me. That scent . . .

    untold ages that wept
    rust-stained hollows
    in the cliffs

Did you read the headstones? Some, she says. What do you think it means? — *the young and strong who cherished noble longings for the strife.* Maybe the War, she says. Although he died in 1887 . . . Did you notice all the children's graves?

  winter sunlight creeping across cracked marble camellias

We wander back down through the cemetery, past an old fire place where sooty stones still testify to the flame once kindled here. It stands apart in the bush, one great stone built up of humbler stones. It is all that remains of the old church that doubled as a school house, damaged in violent storms and finally destroyed by bush fire.

    now the earth has turned
    its back only knows the pale
    warmth of the sun

At the bottom we sit a while on a wooden bench, built on an ancient shell-midden, looking out from the sinking remains of generations. At the end of the jetty our little boat is tied, waiting.

  a kingfisher's thread of mud-and-oyster crusted rocks

The Boat Shed
(for Els)

> *Now the serpent was most cunning...*
>
> — Genesis 3:1

I might scramble up the hill out the back.

Ok, I say, squeezing her slender hand without lifting my eyes.

On the day-bed, a water-mirrored tide of cloud-diffused light bathes the broad timbered sill, the page, and a soul stiff with age. My silent reading of another, found on a stranger's shelf, becomes aloud:

The memories of childhood have no order...[1]

> beyond the shimmering
> spotlight of the moon
> a channel beacon   blinking

---

1. From 'Reminiscences of Childhood' by Dylan Thomas.

The Secret River

> ... *Why*
> *wouldn't I infest this place, where the*
> *sun shines on settlers and their heirs ... ?*
>
> — Robert Adamson, 'Thinking of Eurydice at Midnight'

On the way home we turned off at Mooney Creek to visit Juno, an old friend of my wife's — or my wife's late mother — that she'd known since she was a kid. I was interested to meet her partner, though, the poet — as I'd recently discovered — whose book *The Goldfinches of Baghdad* I'd read some years before. But it was somewhat disappointing: Juno greeted us warmly offering us a cup of tea, chatty and happy to see us; Bob emerged after a little while and while he made an effort to be amiable, seemed distracted . . . Before we got too settled, though, Juno rose, put her cup in the sink, and announced she wanted to show us something. Bob took the cue and slipped out of the room, but reappeared with some books, scrawled something in a copy of what he described as his "latest", *The Kingfisher's Soul*, before handing it to Juno.

We drove at first — well, I drove, Juno directed; and then we walked. It's a sacred place she said, leading us through the bush with her camera in her hand. It's around here somewhere . . . Look for a big flat shelf of stone. We found it before too long littered with leaves and bark debris. Outlined figures began to emerge, carved deep in the stone, resembling a band of flying fox. She took some photos, telling us the little she knew before leading us a little further on to another large rock on the edge of a plunging gorge. From our perch we witnessed a glint of pristine river, just visible, like a snake, way down in the valley.

    evening star the fruit bats set out again

still waters
figuring the mist
morning sun

Repetition 490

"The woman whom you gave by me, she . . ."
— Genesis 3:12

Today over coffee he brings it up again. I listen long enough to know where it's going. You've told me this before. He's annoyed. You haven't let me finish. I let him finish. When he's finished I tell him he's told me before. Have I? Yes, I tell him. A dozen times. I know what you're getting at. What do you mean? — That Mum's a liar, a thief, unfaithful, "like her mother" . . . a despicable person, basically. I wouldn't say despicable, he says. I wonder if he knows what it means. He was never good with words. Always said so himself. Better with numbers. Dad, I love you, but what good will it do bringing it up now? It's been years. I just want to know the reason, he says. But I know that isn't really the reason. Even if she were to admit what you say is true would it make a difference? Depends. On what? He looks down at the newspaper on the table in front of him. Pokes it with his pen. Forget about it. I shouldn't have brought it up. I won't bring it up again.

> seventy times seven
> he begins a new
> sudoku

gibbous moon folding the dew softened washing

Anec-dotage

> *. . . give me property among you for a burying place, so that I may bury my dead out of my sight.*
> — Genesis 23:4

He would yak for hours if I let him, though today I don't feel put upon. To tell the truth I'm kind of glad he dropped in, I needed an excuse, and I haven't seen him in a while. He's been away in Townsville visiting my sister, so he has a bit of news. But before long settles back into his usual repertoire. As he moves seamlessly from one story to the next, I remember this man — who seemed so dauntless and capable to me growing up — is barely literate. — Alas, the limitations of the voice: when the saying ceases, the sound and significance slip back again into that vast silence; the speaker has no ground in such abyss, no purchase in the great memory — or lesser memories . . . compelling reiteration . . . Perhaps that is why he tells his stories over and over and over again . . . perhaps being bound by the same short-comings I write . . .

>   potted succulents
>   my father's on-going eulogy
>   for his mother

air raids begin
tremors in the scroll
of the Zantedeschia

Circles

It is by constantly turning round and round and pressing back the walls on every side, that it succeeds in forming this circle.

— Jules Michelet, in Bachelard *The Poetics of Space*

It's nearly two months since it started swooping again by which I gather she's chosen the same place for the second year in a row.

> somewhere
> in the realm of her vigilance
> a hidden nest

Startled me out of my wits one morning while I was walking. Made two more low passes — the downdraft buffeting the hair on my head — before she was satisfied I was beyond her circle of care. Made me realise: another year...

> season of the goshawk — swoop

I've taken to choosing a stick each time I approach her newly drawn circle, and to walking with it above my head like an antenna. On humid days I use it as well to cut away webs criss-crossing the track. For the first month or so it continues swooping despite my stick, but knowing the hawk's renowned eyesight I figure this will discourage direct physical contact. I had hoped in time she would see I mean no threat, but it seems the instinct is so ingrained, so indiscriminate; and she continues treating me as any common predator. Yet I persist undeterred, though somewhat warily, along the little bush trail where I have taken my morning walks for many years now.

> morning contrails another circle round the sun

In the last week or so I have not been swooped. There's been some blustery weather as late spring temperatures rise — and some big storms. Seeing how the branches are being thrashed about I wonder if her nest has been destroyed. But hope her young are already fledged. Nevertheless I've persisted with my stick-choosing routine. Until today when I figure it's probably safe again, and enter the realm unprotected. But some way in I feel suddenly uneasy and turn — the tilt of wings — aligning — and duck as the feathered *whoop* of her pinions pass close to my head. I look up again and see her wheel and return to a branch high in a tall gum tree where she lets out an imperious piercing titter that makes her whole body quiver.

> editing a reply email
> to my daughter's mother
> a willie wag-tail's night call

spring winds
the jacaranda
in tatters

After All (the King's Men)

*"And when I found the door was shut
I tried to turn the handle but—"*

— Lewis Carroll, *Alice in Wonderland*

*And he ... set up east of the garden of Eden the cherubim ...
to guard the way to the tree of life.*

— Genesis 3:24

It's not the same, not like reading to a child. I noticed she'd withdrawn to her room and when I came looking she said, You don't read to me anymore. Move over then, I said, noticing the book beside her on the bed. I just thought you'd feel you were too big for this kind of thing now. I opened the book and began reading ... but before long she jumps at the sound of something smashing and rushes out to see what it is. When she returns her eyes are avoiding me. She's trying to hold back tears. My step-son is berating himself in the kitchen. I lay aside the book, lower my eyes to her arm, and stroke it softly. She goes to speak and can't. She's trying to explain why she gets so upset whenever something shatters: Even if it's not something I care about, she says brokenly, I still cry.

silica sparkles in stone cicadas

rain rings patterning the low flying swallows

Hiatus

> rain on the café window
> still as buildings
> battleships

On route to the job I enter the Harbour tunnel and begin to descend. Perhaps the caffeine or perhaps going under puts me in the subjunctive mood: what if a bomb exploded, part of the tunnel collapsed engulfing us in our cars . . . cars like bubbles . . . water pressing at every window . . . separated . . . each from the other — in front, behind, beside, each imprisoned in our own capsule, with someone else, or alone. Death imminent and certain as it could possibly be with maybe only minutes or seconds . . . What if I make one last call . . . would it get through . . . or go to her voicemail. What would I say. Still driving I catch myself mentally rehearsing the message I'd leave my wife, my daughter, my . . .

> light at the end . . .
> please leave a short
> ten second message . . .

electrical wires in the storm dishevelled nest

Trigger

For sevenfold Cain is avenged,
And Lamech seventy and seven.

— Genesis 4:23

While she's showering I slip into bed enjoying the feel of fresh sheets and wait listening to her movements anticipating her body's naked flesh hearing the water shut off the shower door removing my last piece of clothing my fingers find the little tear in the neck of this old T-shirt and I see him again pull out across on-coming traffic in front of me the bloody idiot hitting the horn the brakes the screeching to a halt out of his car storming towards me reaching through my window grabbing me what the fuck you blow your horn my indignation his spitting me barely noticing her slip in her touch finding leaving me frozen cut off in clenched fury playing out secret alternate violent endings . . .

>moorhen foraging
>around the reeds
>distant traffic

here without being here in the forest

Happy Days

> "... and they shall be signs for the fixed times and for days and years..."
>
> —Genesis 1:14

When I come in from work my step-son is the only one home. He calls out "Hello" so I poke my head into his room. Pink Floyd's *Animals* is playing and he's keen to tell me about it. There's a pile of old records on his bedroom floor that my Dad brought over for him the night before, knowing he's into "vinyl" at the moment. On the top of the pile I notice *Rock Around the Clock*, by Bill Haley and his Comets, and pick it up. "Wow, I'd forgotten about this. Dad, used to play it sometimes when we were kids."

While he monologues about which album he's planning to buy next I turn the sleeve over and scan the brief bio on the back: Bill Haley was part of a popular group called "Down Homers" ... started his own group "Bill Haley's Saddlemen", then "In 1952 the group changed their name to the 'Comets'...."

Noticing he'd lost me he changes tack: "You know when David Gilmour was asked what made him decide to play guitar, he said: that *Rock Around the Clock* came out when he was ten probably had something to do with it." "Really?" I say. "Yeah, apparently that song was like an anthem for rebellious youth in the 50's. Kind of like *Another Brick in the Wall* was when you were at school." "That's interesting—but right now I'm more interested in soaking in a hot bath with my book," I say, flinging the record back on the pile...

I lower myself into the steaming water with a glass of wine and an abridged edition of *The Gulag Archipelago*, remove the bookmark, take a sip of wine, and settle to reading Chapter 11, 'Tearing at the Chains', in Part V, 'Katorga': ". . . At peace and at ease on our familiar bunks, in our familiar sections, we greeted the new year, 1952. Then on Sunday, January 6, the Orthodox Christmas Eve, when the Ukrainians were getting ready to observe the holiday in style — they would make kutya, fast till the first star appeared, and then sing carols — the doors were locked after morning inspection and not opened again. . . ."

fog lifting the police tape across a house in our street

night train slowing to the station crickets

Sleepwalkers

Under the gypsy moon,
She is observed by things there,
Things she cannot see.

— Lorca, 'Somnambulist Ballad'

Many stars lined up
hoping you'd notice.

— Rilke, 'First Elegy' in *Duino Elegies*

We are housed — now — in a dream. Sheltered from the starry heaven, the daystar, the gypsy moon. If we run, we run between shelters and dream — what we remember — senseless dreams of green and the silver moon. Even she is lost for a time in the fluorescence of a thousand little street-lighting moons. But no-one walks there. The pristine redolence of the little stars that light our rooms, dimmed in those to whom they were bequeathed. We dug in . . . now our tunnelling is ramified, a thousand radical, a thousand virtual, a thousand vicarious dreams. We entertain no angelic beings, nor permit intercourse with greater existences; only with those of our own deciphered world. If we go out it is sap-like into our thousand branchèd tree; but we do not ascend, not really; we never leave the mythic cavern. Language too, the ancient serpent, sold us eyes at the price of seeing. — But look!

> below the balcony
> a thousand silver moons
> in the money tree

here today
gone tomorrow
cactus flower

Stanmore Video

Lot's wife . . . looked back . . .. Abraham . . . looked down . . .
— Genesis 19:26-28

It's a bottle shop now. We used to come here every week after I'd pick her up from her Mum's. The anticipation excited her, I think. — I always let her choose a video, and a little treat from the goodies on the counter . . . or an ice cream from the freezer in summer. It happened every time . . . The staff were good about it. After a while I didn't have to ask. When he saw us come in Charlie just gave a little smile and put the toilet key on the counter . . .

These days she's in her room mostly, preferring Snapchat or Skyping friends to watching movies with her old man . . .

>streaming issues . . .
>a couple of beers
>with the balcony moon

what to do with her cicada shells

Confinium

> *... I made cloud its clothing,*
> *And thick mist its swaddling bands ...*
>
> — Job 38:9

In the afterglow I suggest we drive to Little Bay to see the sun rise. So we take General Holmes Drive — the southern overpass with its brief vista of the airport — its vigilant lights anticipating the dawn — then dive under the runway. We turn right onto Foreshore Road — along the reclaimed northern shore — past Port Botany — the remains of the industrial zone — then right onto Bunnerong Road . . .. But the sun is there before us.

We stroll down past the A-frame chapel at the top of the cliff, across the narrow neck of the golf course to the stairs descending to the beach. The sun itself cannot be seen: heavy cloud hanging just above the horizon is hiding it from view. But its radiance is not concealed: shards of golden light splay down from its hidden source, flooding the gap between the solid slab of cloud and the dark, slightly wrinkled rim of the horizon, casting the silhouette of a distant ship at its centre into vivid relief — like a stage set, so neat and luminous — drawing the eye out to the edge of the world.

We descend the wooden stairs, greeting a group of elderly towel-caped bathers that are talking on the landing. The tide is high. Three men, evenly spaced, are fishing from the beach. The sea is roused, pushing through the throat in strong sets, spilling up the beach of the bay's retort. Barefooted, we skirt the shore; its coarse shelly sand, riddled with fragments of coloured glass and broken crockery, hurts our feet. At the southern end a little track leads out, over rocks, and up to the headland.

We emerge on the battlements, as it were, overlooking the vast plain of the sea, and sit under the luminous shadow, watching. Advancing formations six or seven deep rise ominously to their full stature, before plunging, shattering themselves against the wall of rock at our feet. A furious spume unnerves us, a warning that we are not beyond reach — as deep tremors ring the huge turret of stone on which we have staked our safety. But between each assault we dare to lift our eyes: the little snail-ship progressing like a minute-hand along the rim of the world, tinges of goldish-green mingle in contours of the cloud's dark violets . . .

What are you thinking? she says . . .

> still nothing
> in the fisherman's bucket
> the face of a man

rock overhang
a bush spider sieves
the soft morning breeze

Sphinx

Write in a book what you see...

— Apocalypse 1:11

Fire too can harness the wind. These past weeks have seen the bulging spinnakers. The smell, the gauzy haze infused through everything. From Kirribilli I watch the stealthy veil envelop the City. On the far shore the babel of buildings fade, confuse, vanish: ... the ferries in the Quay ... a titanic cruise ship. By 10 O' Clock all engulfed ...

A foghorn sounds ...

In the smoke-dimmed tide the Opera House transforms: instead of sails, pale hooded heads, monk-like, *somewhere in sands of the desert*, watching, praying. One dull-glowing coal-like eye, a smoke-tarnished sun-glint. The once optimistic parabola of the Bridge falling to the shore of an anxious abyss ...

>   dipping its nib
>   in the ink of the creek
>   summer swallow

hedge fund
the financial advisor's
odd hand shake

Excursion

What immortal hand or eye
Could frame thy fearful symmetry?
— William Blake, 'The Tyger'

Freedom from fear has arrived, but a glory had departed from the green lagoons.
— Aldo Leopold, *A Sand County Almanac*

It's a sweltering summer afternoon. The whole family, indoors, languidly absorbed in devices, tolerating the ineluctable heat and bushfire smoke. "Did you see this report about fires so intense they create their own weather," someone says. "The media's a fire that creates its own weather," I say, scrolling, recalling, for whomever cares to listen, some of the "doomsdays" that have come and gone in my lifetime. Then this: "Ancient Tree Discovered with Record of Earth's Magnetic Field Reversal in its Rings." . . . In New Zealand . . . under 26 feet of soil . . . during excavation for expansion of a geothermal power plant . . . Agathis Australis . . . 'Kauri' to the Maoris . . . 8 feet in diameter and 65 feet in length . . . carbon dating showing it lived 1,500 years, between 41,000 and 42,000 years ago . . . its lifespan covering a time "when the magnetic field almost reversed." Almost?! Now I'm interested. What causes these 'reversals' anyway? What could they mean for us . . .? A few more searches gives me to understand there are a few theories . . .

> brightening a neighbour's
> fake flower garden
> summer rain

the limited life of our sacrificial anode

Holiday Reading

*Water and fire shall rot
The marred foundations we forgot*

— T. S. Eliot, 'Little Gidding' in *Four Quartets*

I drop easily — as any child bred on Australian beaches — beneath the predictable battery of another glary, frothy set — and at the last, expect to surface comfortably within the ample measure of a breath . . . but the face of the bright world is not there to kiss me . . . I thrust upward, seeking the elusive air — panicked, wringing my every last fibre of its breath . . . and break the surface of viscous slumber into the expansive air, relief.

My vision blear, the air bright, and still wet with sleep, I close again, my eyes and become aware of the book splayed open on my belly, my thumb still separating the parched labia at the place I slipped away. On the creased and wrinkled sheet, several more in varying states of disarray, some tattooed with fine henna, track notes, tasting notes, marginalia of a search for meaning, of intercourse with inscribed souls. The faintest incarnation of a smile, the echo of a passing recollection, of my wife's mock protestations at such flagrant indiscretions, at being expected to share her bed with my 'lovers'. The ceiling fan stirring the hot air, the sensation of its soft buffetings. My eyes wander listless among the ruins, the buckled ground, a broken column, the spiral pillars and piles around the room, toppled, leaning, shelves upon shelves, a library once, a temple, now dishevelled stone. These tangible remains of a once enticing illusion, parchments of exhausted ideals, inheritance and wages — both — of a sin. A vice Heaney must have known. How did he put it? — speaking of Eliot's 'Little Gidding': ". . . shimmering with the promise of revelation . . ."

    bushfire
    in the membranes, beach sand
    in the bed sheets

touching the length
and breadth of the creek
a duck's wake

on my desk a clipping of your fingernail moon

The Possum Shift
(for Saffron)

I'm woken by the possum again. Its entry point into the roof is just above our bed. For almost a year it's been waking me well before dawn. Annoying at first. I'd try, but could never get back to that dreamless sleep. My body clock inversely synchronised with its routine — waking me at the time it's going to sleep. Lately I've come to see it is a strange sort of gift — leading me like a blind man to the hours hallowed for writing. So now, when the possum comes in I get up while everyone is still asleep and wash my face, put the kettle on, and make myself a cup of tea. Before getting down to it I step out into the back yard to greet the moon and the stars and see what they're are up to. The Milky Way is not visible — too much light pollution — let alone the Dark Emu . . . But the good old Saucepan is there, and the Southern Cross. We're about to enter the time of the dark moon . . . Strange. It always seems when you're here we're both busy or preoccupied. You're a bit like the possum, or I am. I know you're almost an adult, but still, there it is . . .

> the ache of your absence
> in the firmament
> my heart

hanging washing
in moonlight
jasmine

Bird Watching

It's early. Most of the shops in the dim-lit mall are still not open. I place my order and stand back to wait. A flash of light draws my attention — to a young woman, waiting to be served at the coffee counter. She has shapely well-tanned legs, framed nicely by her short white shorts and white heeled ankle-boots. Her high waisted black leather jacket draped about her shoulders. Before I'm able to home in on the exact source, it flashes again — then again. She turns slightly, deflecting reflections from her screen, and I realise by the waist-height position she's holding her phone, she's taking shots of her own legs . . . perhaps her boots. She spends some time choosing the filter she wants before the woman behind the counter repeats, Next please.

> blue satin
> he brings to the bower
> the colour of her eye

pillow creases
on her cheek
a vase for the poppies

Pietà

Take your son, your only son Isaac, whom you love . .
— Genesis 22:2

After a cold shower, we remove the pile of presents from the bed, throw back the covers and lie down naked, silent at first, watching the ceiling fan slowly turning, feeling the slight breeze caressing our sweaty skin.

I heard on the radio that tonight is going to be Sydney's hottest December night since 1858, my wife says.

Maybe, I say, watching the fan. It's too hot to sleep.

You're popular, I say, nodding at the pile of presents.

Yes. After our Christmas show today, the father of one little girl told me that when he gets home in the evenings his daughter makes him play with her: You be Els, she says, and makes him play the games she played that day with me. And when she's had enough she says, Mummy's here to pick me up now. Bye bye.

It's nice that he'd feed that back to you, — how significant you are in his daughter's life. I mean, some parents might be jealous for their children's affections.

I don't think I've told you, when I first got the position they said they'd been looking for someone with children of their own, since most of their educators and carers were young single women, or young married women with no children, and no real experience of being a parent. And I guess it is easier for me to understand what it might be like for some parents: entrusting the little person at the centre of their lives to others each morning and walking away . . . — especially for a mother who has borne that little person inside her own body.

You should see some of the gifts . . .

> a handmade card
> *unto us*
> *a child is born* . . .

mangrove light
a place the dove song
has taken me

Strange Feather

> *... and every winged bird of every kind. And God saw that it was good.*
>
> — Genesis 1:21

A couple of weeks ago I noticed a Pekin duck foraging along the shallow edges of the creek. I've seen it a couple of times now. This morning, here it is again. To a visitor it might seem nothing strange, being a duck and all. But to a native eye it would seem rather an oddity. There are three species endemic to the area: the Australian Wood Duck, the Pacific Black Duck, and the Chestnut Teal. It strikes me as funny and a bit sad — this big white Pekin tagging along with a bunch of Black Ducks, trying to act casual, one of the gang, as if there were nothing wrong with this picture, but not quite carrying it off. Its manners and movements are all very ducky of course, but among this low-key bunch it seems ungainly and comical, like a new kid trying a little too hard to make friends by wearing a clown suit on his first day. I wonder where it came from, where it roosts at night, will it find a mate . . .

> parent teacher night
> the-kid-on-the-spectrum's
> mother in tears

afternoon birdsong
the fishbone fern
brush my knees

Pedestrian Crossing

... and they knew that they were naked ...
— Genesis 3:7

I had to stop for an ibis on the way to work this morning. I mean, it wasn't really a choice — to stop or not. The law is the law, right? And technically it was on foot — despite possessing the power of flight. It seemed haughty, though, supercilious. Something about the way it walked: measured, self-conscious, almost defiantly unhurried, as if it knew its rights and was, in the way it walked, stating the fact. Was it mocking? Were a human being to cross in such manner would we not say she's 'putting on airs' or he's 'pushing his luck'? But this was a bird . . . On second thought: perhaps that slightly excessive 'taking its time' was the manifestation of a concealed tentativeness — the partial paralysis or stiltedness produced by the hyper self-consciousness of feeling one is out of one's element but wanting not to seem so, wanting to appear perfectly normal and casual . . . yet coming across as ridiculous, pretentious, a parody of both casualness and normality?

> jay walker
> the homeless man
> flaunts his liberty

serenity prayer
the reach
of the white necked heron

Wild Mountain Scene

... and they sewed fig leaves ...
— Genesis 3:7

Trees don't make excuses, never get ahead of themselves, are not anxious. Trees don't fall into what the desert fathers called *accidie*, that first symptom of 'the sickness unto death'. They simply accept their conditions — absolutely pure of heart, they will one thing — and so effortlessly, inadvertently, and with seeming infinite patience transform those conditions. Trees have always been exemplary teachers in this respect, and a great comfort to human beings. If only I were more like one of these trees... Such are the thoughts that lift like clouds from the valleys of my mind as I contemplate a stand of junipers growing vertically, straight as arrows, an improbable little family in a lush mossy bed on a slab of stone . . . fallen — one imagines — from a cliff above . . . somehow coming to rest pitched like a roof at forty five degrees.

> poised in the stark space
> of the bonsai table
> a fawn

The Tower

... You speak
all languages and none,
answering our most complex
prayers with the simplicity
of a flower, confronting
us, when we would domesticate you
to our uses, with the rioting
viruses under our lens.

— R. S. Thomas, 'Praise'

On my way home on Friday afternoon the City was almost deserted because of lockdown. I was driving west down Broadway when the lights changed and I stopped. My attention was drawn to the 'peeling' façade of the UTS Faculty of Engineering and Information Technology building. The impression amused me. I took a photo with my phone and, at the next red light, posted it on Facebook with the caption, "The sides are starting to peel off this building." A few people reacted or commented. A couple expressed their liking for the building. One recalled that "the grill", as it is commonly known, "is actually a binary code", but couldn't remember what it meant . . . I found myself wondering whether this was symptomatic or symbolic of our 'post-modern condition': — Now that our cities — our mega-cities — have become overwhelmingly complex, what Aristotle said somewhere about the population limit of the ancient *polis* being determined by the number of citizens that can gather within ear-shot of a crier makes one nostalgic for a simpler world . . .

We've long since exceeded the limit of our individual capacity to comprehend the technologies upon which we now depend, and which now mediate virtually every facet of our relation to the world. But I have moments . . . like Goethe's aversion to the symphonies of Beethoven which, rather than finding sublime, he felt to be clamorous amalgamations of sounds wherein individual instruments and voices were no longer distinguishable as they still were in the music of Bach . . . The car behind me beeped, the light had changed . . .

>humming tree
>the teetering dandelion's
>slow explosion

Lockdown Mullet

"Come into the ark, you and all your household..."
— Genesis 7:1

Before the Delta variant reached our golden shores my daughter asked if she could give me a mullet, — like the one her cousin had given himself to impress his mates. Wanting to preserve some shred of parental dignity I politely but firmly declined. But now, after a couple of months of increasing restrictions I've had a change of heart: perhaps it will be a bit of fun, good for morale. I tell the kids, OK, anything goes, then light a fire in the backyard burn-barrel and make myself a Stonewall: three parts peaty scotch, one part triple sec, fresh squeezed lemon juice, marmalade, shaken, strained over ice. I set up my camping chair near the fire and brace myself for the worst haircut of all time.

    pines soughing
    the tonsured head
    of a dandelion

Niche

> *At the end of forty days Noah opened the window of the ark ...*
>
> — Genesis 8:6

A smatter of raindrops shaken from needles of a she-oak. Turning just in time to see a Rock Warbler flitter off. I stand a while, admiring the light distilled by the night rain: tiny droplet jewels clinging to the needle-tips, adorn the deeper milky lichen-green of the branch on which all are delicately depending. Faint rings expanding seemingly from nothing — like blown bubbles, bursting — appear like a pattern across the surface of the creek. Probably only a passing shower, but it gets me moving —

> rock shelter
> through the valley drizzle
> an outbound train

jacarandas bluing the storm grey dawn

Radical Feminist

The last of them clambers over the fallen branch obstructing the way to the rock-ledge which overlooks a pleasant bend in the creek where I sometimes like to sit. They stand in a clump blocking the narrow track, a group of them, late teens — early twenties maybe, two guys and three girls; fresh, slim, good-looking. Something homogenous about their physique and style of dress — casual but new, well-fitted jeans, displaying no blatant branding — from seeming well-to-do families. "Which way do we go?" one of the guys says — as if speaking for them both, "We don't know where we are." One of the girls steps forward to take the lead — and sees me waiting to get by. We regard one another momentarily. "Hi," I say, smiling — my eyes drawn to the words written in stark white letters across the chest of her dark blue top . . . I continue on my way wondering what she might have said if I'd asked about her adjective . . .

> twilight deepens
> soft cries from a hollow
> in the spotted gum

Woman with Beard

Beauty is . . . the unity of the psychic and the somatic.
— Kierkegaard, The Concept of Anxiety

Most ineluctable — despite the veil, the 'curtain' of beard — are the eyes — windows of a soul. Isolated. Concentrated in the frames and panes of her spectacles, they wait, like a Coptic icon, watching. Her halo flat, a hat — though crushed or bowed — suggesting perhaps, along with her pained brow, an invisible burden. Her posture strong, though, like a tree — seeming all-the-more-so for the beard. But her eyes, *once seen*, like St Anthony's — transfixing painter and viewer alike with their directness, intelligence, long-suffering — are also seeing . . . Who witness the transfiguration — the contradiction — this *one from whom men hide their faces* suddenly auraed with dignity? L. S. Lowry saw her — "an able and intelligent woman, completely alone and isolated behind her deformity" — bearing witness in his painting to her invisible beauty — in the paradox of her well-groomed beard. — Saw she did not despise it — did not shave or neglect it — but in the desert of her own ab-normality learned the meaning of the desert Abba's word: "Sit in your cell and give your body in pledge to the walls."[1]

> cliff swallows
> cribbed high a crevice
> a fig

---

1. *The Wisdom of the Desert Fathers: Systematic Sayings from the Anonymous Series of the Apophthegmata Patrum* (trans. Benedicta Ward SLG), #73.

a water hen scours
the trampled reeds
wafer moon

Amma Sarah's Unseen River

> magpie song
> breaching the blind
> before the light

Those that rise before the sun — to take their lockdown exercise along this path, — that have shut their ears to the voice of the river . . ., — the earbuds and headphones — do not hear the birds chanting lauds regardless in the monastery of trees. I recall this word of Amma Sarah, the desert mother: "It was said concerning her that for sixty years she lived beside a river [the Nile] and never lifted her eyes to look at it."[1]

> cloud blush sky deep in the dawn river

I've been acquainting myself with the desert fathers and mothers since the pandemic began, mainly the *Apophthegmata*, the 'sayings'; just a page or two each day. Fleeing to the desert, so to speak, has affected me in unexpected ways. I thought to find their asceticism impertinent in this day and age, objectionable even. And like much desert asceticism Sarah's practice did seem senseless at first — a pointless denial, pathological even. A religious of all people surely is permitted to take joy in the sight of a river — as a gift of God.

> mangrove sun warming the mud bristles

---

1. *The Sayings of the Desert Fathers*, 'Sarah', #3.

But listening to the birds, I realise: to not lift one's eyes to look at the river one must be aware of the river — precisely because one lives by it. For more than twenty years I've lived beside Cooks river and only now — contemplating your way of life — do I begin to understand there is more than the *ineluctable modality of the visible* — the glamour that meets the eye . . . Did averting yours enable you to apprehend it more fully . . . in other senses . . . magnify it even? — That you lowered your eyes — as when a stranger's eye meets our gaze — signify that shame — that, in knowing it is seen, is reminded of its nakedness . . . of the one that *flows out of Eden* . . .?

>river light
>beneath the native she-oak trees
>a mulberry bowed down

broken bough   the hollow of a dove's egg moon

The Street View Gallery

... And all things were her sleep.
— Rilke, Sonnets to Orpheus

I don't know how many times I drove past before I really saw her. I mean I saw, of course, exactly what was there, and liked it, too, somehow. It drew me with its shades of beige and grey, its white and black — its subtle hints of green — its details, lines, use of clean space that blended so seamlessly back into the bland beige wall (on the other side of which someone may well have been making coffee, watching TV, sleeping...). For ages I couldn't quite make it out, like the sounds of a foreign language. The bottlebrush on the verge didn't help — or helped, I should say, by being in the way, piquing my curiosity. Nor did the fact that it was on the corner of a busy roundabout — near the railway line at the end of Liberty. Trying to snatch a glimpse while exiting onto Kingston and keeping an eye on the road at the same time was tricky. And besides the challenging placement of the exhibit, its perspective is unusual. Even when I showed my wife on Google Maps it took her a while. I'm not sure it has a title: I thought, maybe, Sweet Dreams (there is a hint of a smile) or Sleeping Beauty...

> little briar rose
> waking again from the dream
> within a dream

dusk in the heart of the laurel dove song

Daphne

May she become a flourishing hidden tree ...
— W. B. Yeats, 'A Prayer for my Daughter'

On the way to the duck pond her chatter is cheerful, brimming with anticipation of the day's possibilities which she's already singing into being. It's a sunny winter morning, the last day of school holidays, but her sweet heart is still happily overflowing. Her voice is like morning birds; tinkling and incessant as a mountain stream. After we've fed the ducks we play on the swings a while before meandering back home along the creek. She slips her hand in mine and, despite her heart's mythology, says she loves me — though quick to add — I love my real Dad too.

>   shining through the veins
>   of the laurel's crazy leaves
>   winter sunlight

evening star the fruit bats set out again

Kingdom of the Heavens

In a remote area of the Buddewang Ranges I stop for a drink of water and notice a small wildflower quivering in the heath. With nothing demanding my attention I give it to the little flower and wonder . . . out here, has anyone ever noticed its existence.

>   above the flicker
>   of fire-light in the trees
>   countless twinkling stars

    warmer
       pockets
  on the riverbank
   a midge-   veil
     shimmies

        the sound of rain

after rain   rainbows

Been There

You do not find it by travelling but by standing still.
— Thomas Merton, *A Book of Hours*

> moonlight I tell her the scent of wattle blossom

There's something to be said for staying, putting down roots, the rhythm of repetition. I've been walking along this track now for years. Very little changes. Not quickly. Or not when you're looking. Impatience with the natural order devises machines; an indecency that violates the modesty of her tempo with time-lapse reveals.

> adagio a fiddlehead unfurling

Creation's metronome. The implicitness of time. Day and night, the waxing waning moon, the tides and seasons . . . Existence is initiation: the mysteries being-in-time reveals. Almost imperceptibly one grows aware.

> being so the forest enters in

When the time is right — a wet or humid day — a little posse of Eastern Long Neck Turtle claw and clamber up from the creek to lay their eggs along a certain section of the track. The sun's rising and setting through the year, altering ever so slightly — not just position, but disposition — pulls back a veil, disposes one to notice something hidden every other day. Yesterday a house, high on the escarpment, mostly shrouded in trees. Remarkably I'd never seen it there. — Until the morning sunlight in that moment, glancing from a window like a wink, caught my eye ... Yes, something to be said for staying, putting down roots, the rhythms of repetition.

    thick fog I am asked to listen for a change

mist lifting reflections and their swallows kiss

'This Lolita'

*What is beautiful lasts only as long as it is looked upon,
But what is good will soon also be beautiful.*

— Sappho, Fragment 50

To be fair I shouldn't make too much of her response — it'd been more than twenty years since she'd read it; while I, at 51, having lately got around to it, had a still fresh impression. But in the mildly melancholic mood one can find oneself on a Sunday afternoon, approaching the end of a holiday — and, on this occasion, after a good book — I was left feeling an insupportable pity for its narrator ('Humbert the Terrible'), a heart-pang of sympathy for his grief at the loss of the girl who, despite it all (it seemed to me) he utterly adored — and, yes — loved even. Out of this reluctant and still somewhat spellbound state of mind, still clutching the closed book in my hands — as if it contained something unspeakably precious, I became aware of the presence of my wife quietly folding washing at the end of our bed.

   winter sunlight creeping across cracked marble camellias

In the afterglow of *Lolita*, while she was still unaware my attention had turned, I regarded her: the way she moved, the way she held herself, her face with its peculiar contours, lines, complexion . . . trying to discern through time's veil — in the *faint violet whiff and dead leaf echo* — the nubile form of her own nymphet.

   black satin night gown gaping alabaster moon

Do you think Humbert really loved Lolita? She frowned, — perhaps in the realisation I'd been watching her, — perhaps at the preposterous suggestion he *may* have — perhaps at having her own private reverie interrupted, and took some time to answer.

    gibbous moon folding the dew-softened washing

I waited, watching her face with unhurrying expectancy, as her frown took on a shade of irritation, perhaps at my perverse interest in the devil Humbert, perhaps at the unfairness of the question being put to her *now*, perhaps at being obliged to remember details of a self-serving story cooked up by a depraved and objectionable man she would not otherwise have given a second thought, but eventually, and with notable vehemence (let the reader understand), she spoke: No. He only loved himself — his fantasy — which she embodied for a while in her adolescence. But when he finds her again, some years after she'd escaped him, and she's changed — having become a woman — and carrying another man's child — no longer the embodiment of his pubescent ideal — as I recall — he was *nauseated* at how time had ravaged her. No, I wouldn't call that love.

    streetlight my undoing her negligee of venetian shadows

afterglow clifftop silhouettes of slowly swaying trees

Neighborhood

. . . among the trees . . .

— Genesis 3:8

Some nights when the house is all asleep he comes and sits out here on the steps beside us and smokes and sips from a mug of tea. Here he can be and think as if he were alone. A little breeze comes and goes, its passage traced in the rustle of our leaves. Thinks: — *Sometimes trees are the best company. One can be at ease. With them there is no comparison.* And for a moment considers: (us here) — how (seemingly forgotten and neglected) we grow; unobtrusive, constantly, abiding all extremes and variations, unsheltered, enduring, naked witnesses of every season, hidden for the most part in plain sight. — *How close and modest and reassuring they always are.* He takes a thoughtful toke and looks up — exhales, through our latticework of leaves — to the silent stars, and wonders . . . (Perhaps the smoke — disturbs one of our little sleeping birds that mutters something as if in a dream, and settles again.) His ear . . . falling now to the hush of a lone car . . . threading its way through the surrounding suburban labyrinth . . . follows the sound till it fades . . . drinking the last sweet dregs of tea . . .

> between soft thuds
> of palm drupe, night's lull-a-bye
> of crickets

still water
depending on a bent reed
a dew drop

she-oak shadow reaching this sun-baked stone river breeze

evening stars all at once the cicadas cease

Afterword

Although I have an image of myself as writer and poet hanging in my wardrobe, I've been quite reluctant to wear it out. One of my clients asked me recently if I had a hobby. That category, the hobby or avocation, somehow made what probably sounds like an odd interest for a plumber seem more fitting. At the same time I don't want to be falsely modest. Often there is more to a hobby than meets the eye. Aldo Leopold regards a hobby as "a defiance of the contemporary", as "an assertion of those permanent values which the momentary eddies of social evolution have contravened or overlooked." But more pertinent to my dilemma he considers whether, for something to qualify as a hobby, it "must be in large degree useless, inefficient, laborious or irrelevant."[1] Mine certainly ticked all those boxes. But does that mean hobbies are *unnecessary*? Can a thing be both useless and necessary? In the end such questions can only be answered by the hobbyist himself.

Necessity, they say, is the mother of invention. It is also, I would suggest, the mother of compromise. I began working with these short forms — haiku, senryu, tanka, haibun — out of a sort of necessity. The peculiar need to write arose for me, on the one hand, out of the persistent inability of my means of making a living to satisfy or pacify or harness some inexplicable excess in me. I suspect that most people who have hobbies are misfits of one sort or another, ill-bred to the reigning economy; their hobbies the strange fruit of unseasonable trees, individual manifestations of values (this is Aldo's point) unvalued by the greater society. But for me it was not straightforwardly

1. 'A Man's Leisure Time' in *A Sand County Almanac*.

a need to write, or realise writerly ambitions, there were also certain pragmatic considerations. These poems — or, more precisely, the forms my writings came to take — were born of a more mundane necessity: the want of time.

The constraints of my life — of being a father, a husband, a son, a brother, a friend, of running a plumbing business — left precious little time for writing the ambitious books I'd imagined since my youth one day writing. (Bearing in mind that the books I was projecting in possibility aligned at that stage more with what seemed to be, socially, 'appreciating'.) One always assumes 'it'll keep', that the future holds time for those currently less demanding, less urgent things. But the older I got the more responsibilities seemed to increase. And though I persevered in fits and starts I felt it was too pretentious — and a denial of the facts — to call myself a writer. Writers wrote. If I wrote, it was in spasms of inspiration or what often felt like bits of stolen time and that usually resulted in writerly miscarriages. At times I blamed or was tempted to blame my constraints . . . At times I rebelled . . . At times — resigned . . . But nothing really changed, except that a bedrock of resentment formed as day by day I watched my youthful dreams pale and become less and less substantial. And the more I railed the more I seemed to prove the law of diminishing returns. Eventually an unexpected solution came.

If only I'd been able to understand what Mr Antolini was trying to tell Holden Caulfield about knowing "the size of your mind" when I read *The Catcher in the Rye* in high school: "After a while, you'll have an idea what kind of thoughts your particular size mind should be wearing.

For one thing, it may save you an extraordinary amount of time trying on ideas that don't suit you, aren't becoming to you. You'll begin to know your true measurements and dress your mind accordingly."[1] — *After a while*, I did.

Humility is a counter-intuitive virtue. And it is unlikely I would have 'condescended' to writing haiku were it not for a friend texting me his cute little poems while I was convalescing after a hernia operation. I found myself helplessly responding in kind. A sort of (bad) haiku dialogue ensued. But more than that, I began to see how productive I became when working in this more manageable form. I could compose haiku in my head, while walking, or driving — or lying in bed — then text them easily to a friend and get instant feedback.

But the more I worked in/with the haiku form the more I realised that it was not only helping my writing take shape, it was also shaping me. Haiku — the poems — are expressions of a kind of sensibility, a kind of attentiveness, a kind of spontaneity, and in the end a kind of submission. Submission is the condition of possibility — I came to realise — that makes beginning actually possible, including beginning as a writer. And this partly accounts for the title *Genesis*.

For me, haiku — the form and the practice — is — besides silence itself — the most modest, the most unpretentious, the most self-oblative form of poetry, of language itself. A haiku is — like a cicada chrysalis, or the cocoon of a moth caterpillar . . . — a way of using words, not for their own or even the poet's glorification, but as a kind of service to facilitate communion in deeper silence, to

---

1. J. D. Salinger, *The Catcher in the Rye*.

facilitate another's 'seeing', another's be-ing. The word (in haiku) is not an end in itself but a means, a sub-mission. Haiku are liminal devices, modes of transport. There is an embarking and a disembarking, but what happens in between and afterwards is the mystery of the reader's participation and ongoing journey. Once the words have served their purpose they can happily be abandoned like a cicada's shell or a moth's casing . . .

Before discovering haiku I used to write a bit of 'free verse' thinking it was . . . well, — free. But then — I can't remember why — I began writing sonnets. That exercise helped me understand the value of form, how working in and with a traditional form — trying to respect the obligations it required, accepting and trusting its rules and constraints — obliged me to wrestle my thoughts into submission. — That is a symptom of what I mean; — that possessive little pronoun 'my' — that (perhaps) nothing but an inherited habit of speech determines one to arrogate thoughts to oneself as 'mine'. We have become very precious about our 'selves' in this age of individualism. The attitude that flows from this seems to be an ignorant outrage, a mindless defiance at the slightest suggestion there might be value in a little 'pruning' or 'excision', let alone more radical 'amputations'. But bringing 'my' thoughts into submission — submission to a form — often produced surprising side-effects, fortunate accidents. Trying to say something in a different way — so that it would fit the form — frequently pushed me outside those glib or cliched habits of thought or prejudiced patterns of speech and resulted often in an entirely different way of seeing — and thinking about — something. Even more than the sonnet, though, haiku pushes limitation to the nth degree. The haiku brings language to the edge of silence ... to the limen, where it quietly transforms those that are ready and willing ...

Paradoxically, I discovered, 'freedom' is not found in infinite, unbounded, unconditional possibility, despite how liberating that may sound. More and more I found freedom in finitude, in limitation, *actual* freedom, that is. The hardest part in this, however, is the letting go, the relinquishing of all those other tempting possibilities and obligations, and those lines one has become overly attached to, overly identified with. Doing this — the act of letting go — is not unlike what Kierkegaard described as 'a leap'. And the moment one takes the decision — faith becomes a necessity, for no-one knows the future except God, assuming of course God exists, — but that is precisely the point. And whether or not you call it God, one has to put oneself entirely — by which I mean the entirety of oneself, one's future and all of one's subjunctives — in those invisible 'hands' believing, or (if one cannot yet do that) at least hoping, they are good and capable and worthy.

The decision to work with a form is not unlike that; — or like taking vows, a kind of promising or betrothing or pledging oneself. The true religious — those who have 'bound themselves' by the taking of vows — have always understood this. 'Wedding' another is also, understood correctly, a religious (a freely chosen 'binding') state of existence. But positive, decisive actuality, in the broadest sense, is a 'binding' or 'wedding' of oneself to another. It is a form of 'ascesis', an 'exercise'. It has both its Yes and its No. That is the paradox.

This is one sense in which poetry — the act — is an almost perfect analogy of human existence. This is also, I suspect, the hidden reason poetry is one of those ubiquitous human activities. It is a 'poetic' performance of the task, an analogical enactment of the meaning of existence. It is analogical, as Jung has shown, in the way the Magnum Opus of the alchemist's art was analogical. Even if they were seeking literally to transmute base metals into gold, the zealous purity with which they pursued the work cannot be accounted for by mundane greed alone. The energy for the work derived I believe from its uncanny analogical relation or *affinity* with the process of individuation, the work, that is, of becoming oneself.

On the other hand there is a sense in which the work of writing this book has been an analogical avoidance of my real work — the true Magnum Opus of becoming myself. But perhaps more importantly an avoidance of the work of being wholly — undividèdly — present in the life I am given (and have to some extent chosen). Even as an avocation the poet-existence is a questionable one. What can justify this turning aside from life in reflection? And how can one know in advance that the sacrifices one makes — sacrifices often made at greater cost to others (Iphigenia, Isaac, Jephthah's daughter . . .) than to oneself (…one's wife, one's children, one's ageing parents…) — that even the sacrifices of one's own time, energy, and attention will in time be justified? In this vein I am reminded of that poignant account (in *Travelogue of Weather-Beaten Bones*) of how Bashō came upon an abandoned child on the bank of the Fuji river, and after giving it what food he could spare, abandons it again to "the will of heaven". One cannot *know* in advance, one can at best only believe such sacrifices will prove worthy of the price one will willingly pay. And it is more than a matter of 'believing in oneself', though that is part of it. None of us know the future. These hours I have taken to write this afterword might be the last of my life. And then, even if I manage to finish it, who can estimate its value? Is the poet-existence an avoidance of the real work that life has assigned us? Or can it be an aid to intensifying reverence for what is truly worthy? But that is the unsettling nature of it. If nothing else, writing this book — writing itself — has nevertheless been for me a way of coming to a greater understanding of this by way of the analogy of poetry itself, by living — even if only as an avocation — a kind of poet-existence.

Another aspect of this comes to light if we consider the way in which writing is a kind of 'hypocrisy' — a word, incidentally, also deriving from the ancient Greek, denoting a compelling theatrical performance. Act, acting, actuality — the word has ambiguity, multiplicity. The ambiguity is there because we forget theatre too is analogy, that its appeal is also an analogical appeal. A poem can be revealing; but like many things it can also be a mask, the 'persona' an actor wears to convince an audience that is often all-too-willingly complicit in the temporary 'delusion' of the play. But implicit in this concept of the persona is 'the curtain call', which entails the recollection — of the person that was wearing the mask, and of the one that wears it vicariously!

We are not all actors in the strict theatrical sense, but I think it is fair to say we all wear masks — whether borrowed or our own creations — when we are obliged to 'face' the world. This is a great mystery: why it is — how it is — that our confrontation with the world has become so riddled with anxiety? In this theatrical mode of presenting oneself to the world it is tempting to fit our individual selves into types; it is all too easy to form habits, to develop routines or repertoires that become automatic or 'second nature'. But in this, one — again, paradoxically — also loses that self-forgetful, carefree spontaneity that is able to respond openly and unaffectedly to reality, to the immanent logic of one's situation in any given moment.

All this is a long-winded and perhaps superfluous attempt to describe my own experience on "the way of poetry" which Bashō — especially in the haunting preamble of his *Knapsack Notebook* — depicted with embarrassing economy. Nevertheless, the writing of these poems has been an exercise in recollection, an exercise in non-compulsive repetition, in living each new day in a way that is not merely going-through-the-motions. The writing has been an aid — a stage prop — as well as an exercise in awakening again and again to the person behind my masks of habit and routine. That 'person' — some have called it the 'inner self' — that we find, like the "old man" in Chao-pien's classic Zen poem, has been sitting there inconspicuously "in all his homeliness", waiting all along.[1] This is not to say that I have always been conscious at the time that this was what I was doing. (That is why I have called this 'an afterword'.) These poems are sketchy, track

---

1. The complete translation of Chao-pien's four-line poem, quoted from *The Inner Experience* by Thomas Merton, runs as follows:

> Devoid of thought, I sat quietly by the desk in my official room,
> With my fountain-mind undisturbed, as serene as water;
> A sudden crash of thunder, the mind doors burst open,
> And lo, there sits the old man in all his homeliness.

notes of my efforts at attending, at listening, at noticing, at trying to understand the language of ambiguity, of paradox, of that voice at once strange and familiar like the sound of the evening breeze, like wind through mountain pines or river bank casurinas. Sometimes in the strange; sometimes in the familiar. Sometimes like the voice of a vocation, calling me *to* something, a task; sometimes like the voice of an avocation, calling me *away* . . . To some extent I have written these poems in the tradition of Bashō's travel writings, and just as I have often been refreshed and encouraged to begin again each new day by the 'track notes' of pilgrim poets I offer these poems to you, my reader, my fellow pilgrim, in hope they will be refreshment for your journey, an encouragement in your resolution, whether your path goes the way of leaving or the way of staying, the way of estrangement or of homecoming.

acknowledgments

I would like to thank the editors and staff (past and present) of the following publications for their efforts in providing opportunities for publication, for their encouragement, and for their helpful and formative feedback over many years. Many of the haiku and haibun in this collection (or earlier versions of them) have appeared previously in the following: *Red Moon Anthology*, *A New Resonance* 9, *Contemporary Haibun Online*, *A Hundred Gourds*, *Paper Wasp*, *The Heron's Nest*, *Frogpond*, *Modern Haiku*, *Haibun Today*, *Acorn*, *Prune Juice* and *Bones*. In particular, I would like to thank Dr Jacqui Murray and, sadly, the late Katherine Samuelowicz, who produced the Australian haiku journal, *Paper Wasp* (where my first published haiku appeared), Jim Kacian, Bob Lucky, Lorin Ford, Mike Montreuil, Terri French, Simon Hanson, and Ray Rasmussen. I would also like to thank Andy MacLean for starting the haiku fire in me; and lastly, my wife, Els van Leeuwen, one of the best poets I have had the privilege to know, who has tended this fire ever since.

author's note

JONATHAN MCKEOWN lives in Sydney with his wife and three children. He makes a living working as a plumber (like his brothers and his father, and *his* father before him).